go-to guides
for
GUYS™

ABCs
for Expectant
DADS

Written by Todd Barrett Lieman

Dalmatian
P·R·E·S·S™

Dalmatian
P·R·E·S·S

The DALMATIAN PRESS name and logo are trademarks of
Dalmatian Publishing Group, Atlanta, Georgia 30329

GO-TO GUIDES FOR GUYS™: ABCs for Expectant Dads
Published by Dalmatian Press, an imprint of Dalmatian Publishing Group.
Copyright © 2007 by Dalmatian Publishing Group, LLC

Written by Todd Barrett Lieman

Cartoons by offthemark.com
Copyright © Atlantic Feature Syndicate
Used by Permission

The author of this book is not a physician, and the ideas,
procedures, and suggestions in this book are not intended
as a substitute for the medical advice of a trained health professional. All
matters regarding your health or the health of your partner require medical
supervision. Consult your physician before adopting the suggestions in this
book, as well as evaluating any conditions that may require diagnosis or
medical attention. The author and publisher disclaim any liability
arising directly or indirectly from the use of this book.

ISBN: 1-40373-667-7
16027-0407

07 08 09 10 GSP 10 9 8 7 6 5 4 3 2 1

To my parents for showing me the way,
and to Lisa and Kolby for making dreams come true.

—TBL

Table of Contents

Introduction 1

A... 4

B... 8

C 23

D 34

E 40

F.. 44

G 47

H 52

I 59

JK 62

L.. 64

M... 68

N 73

O 77

P.. 80

QR 87

S.. 89

T 100

U 104

V 106

W 108

XYZ 112

Acknowledgments........................... 114

Index.. 116

Introduction

"What the heck have I done?"

That's one of the first reactions I had after sharing the "line on the stick moment" with my wife. When you see that line and know your partner is pregnant, there is (usually) immediate joy. Then fear. Then insanity. Then the questions. What do I do next? Who do I turn to? What the hell is an episiotomy? Will I ever play golf again?

Becoming a father for the first time is an exciting time for any man. As the time passed (and my wife grew), I quickly realized that I didn't know the first thing about pregnancy or what to expect. My wife, on the other hand, started studying for the pregnancy with all the vim and vigor of a Harvard-educated med student. She had magazines, books, Web sites, and friends to turn to, all of which were loaded with what seemed like great information. She was going to be prepared.

As for me? I had no idea what to think or expect.

There was no Fatherhood Bible. No go-to book that every dad reads. And then it dawned on me: We're guys. We don't want to read all the details. We don't want the play-by-play. We know the basics: We have sex, we get pregnant, we get big, we get a baby. I didn't want to read a book by another dad about his experiences. And I really did not want to be told what to think or feel or how to react based on other men's experiences. I wanted a reference guide. Something that I could go to when my wife started throwing around words that I didn't understand. (Be honest: How many of you already know what an APGAR score is? Exactly). I wanted a guide that I could run to after a visit to the OB/GYN, to look up all the words I didn't understand (and there were lots of them). I also did not want something so technical that I needed a medical degree to understand it.

I don't expect you to read this book from start to finish. It's not designed for that. It's designed to help you get through the pregnancy thing (and a few months thereafter), at the precise moments when you need help. This book is for those dads who really want to read as little as possible, but know enough to get by. Keep the book handy. Put it on your nightstand and keep it there as a comforting force. Maybe even steal a peek here and there and wow your wife with all your heretofore hidden knowledge!

Congratulations. You're going to be a dad.

Good luck!

Todd Barrett Lieman

A

ADVICE, UNSOLICITED: You know what they say about opinions and a**holes? Everyone has one. When your partner is pregnant, most of the people with the opinions are the a**holes. There is something about being pregnant that makes people feel as though they have the right to weigh in with unsolicited advice about any range of topics. From breastfeeding to swaddling and from baby products to names—the advice will come fast and furious. And it comes from everywhere: friends, family, the mailperson and, for some reason, all retail salespeople. As men (from Mars), we are prone to ignore most of this advice, but our partners (from Venus) will not only listen to the advice but also assume it's good. The best advice: Walk away while you still can (see They).

AFTERBIRTH: Improper use of the term, "I started to hand out the cigars, afterbirth." No. No. No. New dads make the mistake of thinking that once the kid comes out, they're done. Wrong. Afterbirth is all the stuff that comes out after your kid does (see Placenta). Some say it looks like a very raw steak—but take it from me, you'll never barbecue again if you accept that simile. Frankly, the afterbirth is a disgusting concoction of leftovers that are better left unviewed (see Blood). The afterbirth is your opportunity to either pass out or throw up—anything to get out of that room. On the other hand, the afterbirth provides an opportunity for you to prove that you were a "real man" during the actual birthing part. My advice? Tend to your wife after the birth so as not to get a glimpse.

ALCOHOL/WINE: The jury is out on whether or not pregnant women can safely drink after the first trimester (see Advice, Unsolicited). Whenever a pregnant woman sips a glass of wine in a restaurant, disapproving heads turn, and whispers echo, "She's pregnant!" You need to be careful how you react and comment if your partner wants to have a drink in the third trimester (see Egg Shells). For the most part (and off the record), doctors seem to (mostly) agree that a glass of wine or two per week in the third trimester is fine. Many men choose to refrain from drinking if their wives stop drinking.

ALLERGIES: As if there are not 5,000 other things for you to worry about, the subject of allergies is one that leaves most parents fraught with anxiety. Everyone has heard the story of that one baby down the street who was so allergic to everything that she had a list of four foods she was allowed to eat the first year—and they were all white foods. And, while allergies affect only about 2% of children, the effects can be severe— even hampering the child's ability to breathe (see Anaphylaxis). More common than food allergies are food intolerances, whose effects are less severe—if you call vomiting, diarrhea, and spitting up less severe. Common foods that cause allergies are: cow's milk, wheat, peanuts, tree nuts (walnuts, pecans, etc.), shellfish, eggs, and soy. But there are entire books written about allergies and food intolerances and how to cope with them. Your best bet? Call your pediatrician. He or she is used to getting these kinds of questions from new parents.

AMNIOCENTESIS: During the amniocentesis procedure (or amnio for those in the know), which is done between the 15th and 20th weeks, amniotic fluid is removed by placing a long (long, long, long, long) needle through the abdominal wall into the amniotic sac (see CVS). Once the needle is in the sac, a syringe is used to withdraw the fluid, which is used to test all kinds of genetic stuff. Act strong for your partner and upon seeing the needle be careful not to blurt out what you're thinking (which will likely be something like, "Holy sh*t! Thank God that's not going in me!"). There are quite a few "act strong but turn your head away when it counts" moments during the whole expectant dad experience (see Afterbirth, Birth, Diapers, and so much more it's simply useless to try to list them all). This may be one of the more popular of these moments.

AMNIOTIC FLUID: Simply, it's the stuff your baby is swimming around in. The kid is floating around in this cocktail of proteins, minerals, and other compounds that when withdrawn (see Amniocentesis) can help determine the health (and gender!) of the baby (see Gender, Finding Out).

ANAPHYLAXIS: A severe allergic reaction that can cause difficulty breathing, swelling in the throat and mouth, decreased blood pressure, shock, and even death (see Allergies). There is nothing comforting to say about catastrophes like these. Just hope you never have to deal with this. If you ever suspect this condition, call 911.

ANNOUNCEMENTS: Immediately following the birth of your child, it is expected that you and your partner will send out a birth announcement, which is equal parts, "Hey, look what we did!" and "Hey, send us presents!" The announcement usually includes the birth date and time, birth height and weight, and perhaps a picture of the baby. While the announcement may sound simple, it's actually a tremendously complicated process that often requires input that you really don't want (see Advice, Unsolicited, and In-Laws). If you had any issues over your wedding invitations, if applicable, you will be better prepared to deal with the debate over the announcements.

APGAR SCORE: As soon as a minute after birth, then again at five minutes, your kid will be scored on Appearance, Pulse, Grimace, Activity, and Respiratory Effort. Each of these objective signs can receive 0, 1, or 2 points. The APGAR Score is potentially the very first possible grade that new parents can brag about. "Little Chloe got a great score on her APGAR!" Grandparents, in particular, have been known to want to include the APGAR score on the birth announcements, or better yet— college applications and resumes.

ASPIRATOR (aka Bulb Suction): Newborns don't have hair to keep dust and other annoying particles out of their noses. As a result, you'll need to become proficient with the aspirator. A funny-looking rubber tool with a short tube attached to a big bulb, the aspirator is designed to suck the mucous, boogies (technical term), and snot (another technical term) out of your baby's nose. Be sure to squeeze the bulb before you stick it in your baby's nostril or you will force the boogies back in!

AU PAIR: One of the many childcare options available to new parents is the Au Pair (see Nanny). Many men first heard the term au pair when Tiger Woods married his hottie wife Elin Nordegren, who was previously an au pair. And, for many men, the imagined duties of the au pair have come from Internet porn. Au pair is just a fancy word for "foreign person who lives in your house and takes care of your kid." Most au pairs can be found through various agencies that manage the Visa process, insurance, plane tickets, and other paper work. Despite what you may think before the kid comes along, picking the best-looking Brazilian is not the best option. You will actually want to find someone who takes good care of your newborn.

BABYBJÖRN™: You've seen parents walking around with the kid strapped to their chest, right? The contraption that the kid's head, arms, and legs are popping out from is often the BabyBjörn, though there are a host of other brands to choose from (see Sling). The BabyBjörn is not for those with weak backs (see Exercise), and is an excellent way for dads to get a notion (albeit a misplaced, anatomically all-wrong notion) of what it feels like to actually carry a baby.

BABY BLUES: See Postpartum Depression

BABY BREAST BUDS: (see Big Genitalia). Sometimes an infant girl will come out and have what looks like tiny little boobies developing. These are just effects of mom's estrogen. It usually disappears completely. Don't panic.

BABY CLASSES: It's a good idea to take classes with your partner to help get an idea of what to expect during childbirth and when the kid comes home. Many hospitals and private baby depots offer classes like Lamaze and prenatal yoga for couples, as do private baby depots. You will learn important things such as breathing techniques, massage, labor signs, and most importantly, the various narcotics options available for your partner during childbirth (see Epidural, Morphine). Beware: The classes are tremendously graphic and offer no-holds-barred videos of real-life, human births. These classes also provide the instructors with the opportunity to embarrass you by making you participate in role-playing exercises. Stay strong.

BABY FOOD: Like so many things related to babies, the subject of food causes a stir and great debate (see Breastfeeding). When do you actually start breastfeeding the kid (if applicable)? How long will your partner breastfeed (if applicable)? What kind of formula is best during the first year? Is it okay to supplement breast milk with formula (see Nipple Confusion)? When does the kid start on solid food? Some say four months, others say six months. What do you feed her once the time is deemed just right? What sort of solid food is okay? Do you use organic baby food or are you supposed to make everything from scratch? I want my kid to be a vegan, is that okay? What happens if she accidentally eats the tiniest piece of a peanut (see Allergies, Honey)? When will my head stop spinning with all these damn questions about food? Just eat, dagnabbit, eat! Ask your pediatrician (not your parents or in-laws).

BABY GEAR: Baby Gear is anything and everything "needed" to "properly" outfit your child and his environment. From the lightweight, fold-up, must-have designer stroller that goes in the car to the convertible jogging stroller with cup holder and storage for your iPod to the stroller that can get beat up in airline baggage, you'll need a lot of stuff (see Singleton). There are 18 different types of bouncy seats (vibrating or not? umbrella-seated or not?); 15 different types of butt cream; regular diapers, sleep diapers, pull-ups, and swim diapers; 12 different types of bottles in all sorts of shapes, with all sorts of delivery systems—it's endless (see Mannary Glands). And don't you dare question your partner's choices, regardless of price (see Egg Shells, Nesting). The question that will keep hitting you over the head is: How did your parents and earlier generations, those prone to having piles of children, ever do without all this crap?

BABY PROOFING: No. Not a vasectomy. Baby proofing is the (often futile and always expensive) attempt to make your house safe for your newborn, infant, toddler, etc. Early on, there's not much to do since the kid can't move. But, after the rolling starts, then the crawling begins. Then the walking commences, and most houses are simply accidents waiting to happen. There are a number of ways to make the house safer, including: electrical outlet covers, padding on sharp edges, gates at the top of stairs, removing electrical cords, only allowing the bad wines within the baby's reach, and using locks on all cabinets.

BABYSITTERS: There's a new instinct that kicks in when you have your own child. For whatever reason (some sick cosmic joke, perhaps), making sure your kid is safe and well taken care of becomes more important than making sure that you're "taken care of." Plus, there's that whole reality thing—it's not going to happen. Instead, finding the right babysitter is a grueling interview process. The right person is usually equal parts interview performance, experience, references, and gut feeling. Oh, yeah, even though it may not have occurred to you, boy babysitters do exist. They're called your brother(s), your dad, and your best friend—but only if they have already tried out their babysitting techniques on their own children first. I guess that leaves only your dad you can be sure of—and only you know how that turned out.

BABY TALK, BABIES: Baby talk (see Cooing) is a gift. Just about the time you're ready to drive off a cliff, drop the baby off a cliff, drop your partner off a cliff (see Sleep Deprivation), the kid will look up at you and make some strange sound. And somehow it's the best sound you've ever heard. This adorable noise or series of noises is your reward for days, weeks, and months of sleepless mornings, afternoons, and nights. Enjoy it.

BABY TALK, PARENTS: After the kid starts talking in gibberish, it only follows that you will, too. You'll have complete conversations with your kid. She might utter a string of grunts and coos and engage in interesting facial tics that if seen on anyone else would be cause for concern. You'll respond in kind. Not only that, you will soon be able to add a new skill to your resume: that of foreign language translator. Because, before you know it, you will be translating those sounds, deducing that she's asking for a bottle, a boob, or to watch TV. We've all seen this take place at friends' houses or at a mall. Kid: "Ga gooo da ba mmmm oo ma." Parent: "Oh, you want your bottle?" Live it up. At least she wants your attention right now. As she gets older, she won't want to talk to you at all.

BABY'S ROOM: You may very well be sleeping on a 20-year-old mattress and your dresser has been falling apart since your parents got it for you as part of your sixth-grade bedroom set, but the baby's room will be impeccable (see Nesting). You may wonder why a mattress that is an eighth of the size of yours costs twice as much as yours, or why you need so much furniture for such a little being (see Changing Table, Crib, Glider), but you do. The baby's room isn't so much for your baby as it is for your partner (see Egg Shells). Obviously the kid doesn't care if he sleeps in a $100 crib or a $1,000 crib, but your partner does. After the Seinfeld classic line, "Do ya wanna see the baby?", the second most asked question is "Do you want to see the baby's room?" (If you are British, an Anglophile, or simply full of yourself, you may refer to this room as the Nursery, while praying that Mary Poppins shows up really, really soon.)

BABY-CENTERED WEB SITES: You may not know about these Web sites, but your partner does. They are "Momtopia!" Packed with information, discussion boards, product reviews, pictures, advice and more, these online Meccas are an excellent resource for your partner. It is not, however, for you, Dad (see Invisible). Baby-Centered Web sites can be fantastic resources for learning about the development of your baby (e.g., at three weeks, the kid is the size of a sunflower seed). These Web sites are invaluable for times when your partner doesn't feel the baby kick for two hours, or if your newborn coughs. More importantly, this is also the site that can coax your partner off the ledge (see Hypochondria). However, not all baby-centered Web sites are created equally, and not all their information has been checked by experts. *Caveat emptor.* (Let the buyer beware.)

BACK LABOR: Sometimes the kid moves into a tremendously uncomfortable position (for your partner, that is. Don't worry, you're golden!). The baby makes your partner feel like it's hanging out in your partner's back—instead of in her front. The result is extremely painful labor for your partner (more painful than usual, that is). You have the opportunity (read: responsibility) to be a superstar and offer back rubs, support, and empathy. If you choose to ignore your partner's pain, you will instead have the opportunity to be divorced.

BASSINETTE: Not the last name of a once-hot actress. Bassinette is French for "hoity-toity bed for your kid, which is expensive because it has a French name." The bassinette is simply another expensive piece of "baby furniture" (see Baby's Room) that you "need." It's a small bed that allows your newborn to be rolled around the house or apartment or condo in style. As well, it may be what your little tyke sleeps in during the initial few weeks or months.

BATTERIES: AA, AAA, C, D, 9-Volt, and more—you'll need them all. Until you have a kid, you have no idea how many different toys and "necessities" need batteries (see Bouncy Seat, Noise Machine, Swing, etc.). Everything needs some sort of battery. Some of the toys actually need two or three different kinds. You can never have enough batteries and whenever you're at a store—if you see them . . . buy them.

BED REST: In a perfect world, bed rest would be what you get after the kid is born. In reality, that's the last thing you're going to get (see Sleep Deprivation). Instead, bed rest is what happens when there are complications with the pregnancy. Your partner will have to refrain from any strenuous activity and basically ride out the pregnancy in bed (ironically—this is how she probably got pregnant in the first place). Bed rest is not fun. It's boring. It's uncomfortable. This is another of those "knight in shining armor" opportunities for you. Wait on your partner with a smile. Or incur the wrath. Bed rest is common with multiples (see Hormones, Infertility).

BIB: If you need to read the definition of bib, you're totally clueless and have no business having a kid. What you probably aren't aware of, however, is the wide variety of bibs. There are Velcro® bibs, bibs that tie behind the kid's head, slipover bibs, and disposable paper bibs. They are made of cotton. And vinyl. And terrycloth. And polyester. You'll think that you should have gotten into the bib business!

BIG BABY STORES: Your new Mecca. Although you have likely managed never to step foot in these stores before you got your partner pregnant—you will become quite familiar with them after the line on the stick shows up. Baby superstores have everything your baby needs —and even more that she doesn't. Dads wandering the stores alone receive strange stares from the staff. The smart staff members know that, when in doubt, Daddy always buys the biggest, baddest, most expensive item he can find—whether the baby needs it or not (see Competition).

BIG GENITALIA: Don't get excited, we're not talking about you here (see Invisible). Many babies, due to the hormones coursing through their mothers' bodies—and thus their bodies through the umbilical cord—have what seem to be huge genitals, totally out of proportion to their bodies. While your son may be a clone of his daddy, chances are his genitals will become proportional to his body as he grows older. This goes for the girl babies as well.

BIRTH CANAL: When you were in elementary school and learning about the birds and the bees, pictures of the birth canal were as close to porn as you got. Assuming your kid is born vaginally (see C-section) and assuming all goes well, she will descend headfirst, face down, out of the one thing, into the other thing, and out the last thing. Okay, sing along: the birth canal leads from the uterus through the cervix, vagina, and vulva. During this wild ride (see Labor), the kid will get tremendously misshapen. Don't be alarmed (see Conehead, Fontanel).

BIRTH COACH: That's supposed to be you (see Lamaze). Try not to forget all of the breathing and massage techniques that you learned in your classes (most of which you probably never absorbed well enough to practice because you were too weirded out by the videos they were showing, not to mention some of the other couples in your class). Just remember these all-important questions, "What do you need, honey?" Or "Can I get you anything honey?" A favorite, "You're doing great, honey!" If you give any inclination that what happens in the delivery room is about you and not your partner, you might think about making your first call to an attorney and not your in-laws.

BIRTHMARK: You likely know what a birthmark is. But did you know that it's usually the result of a mole or collection of small blood vessels? What's that? You don't care? Didn't think so. Your kid may come out with some strange marks on her head, back, neck, leg, or wherever. We've all got them. It's just that when it's your kid, you may be annoyed that she's not "perfect." Count the fingers. All there? Do the same for the toes? Got 10? Don't worry about it. Many birthmarks may actually go away after a couple of years.

BIRTH WEIGHT: (see Opportunity Weight). This is the weight of the baby when he is born. Not a measurement of how much you gained during the pregnancy. The average weight for a newborn in the U.S. is 7.5 pounds, though many lose a pound or two after birth and gain it back in the first two weeks.

BIRTHING ROOM: It is what it says it is. This is where the magic happens. Well, it's on one of the places where the magic happens. Although, unless you have an at-home birth, it's probably really far away from where the original, real magic happened. Once in the hospital with your partner properly medicated and comfortable, you will end up in the birthing room, which is where you will have your baby. Unless, of course, your partner has a C-section, then the baby will be born in an operating room. Regardless of where the kid is born, your partner will be moved to a recovery room, before finally being moved to the regular room. How much recovering actually happens in there is up for grabs, but they have good pain meds in there.

BLOOD: The red stuff that you may have glimpsed here and there is nothing compared to what you will likely see when your partner gives birth. And no one tells you that your wife will continue to bleed for up to six weeks after the birth—copious amounts of blood. Grin. Bear it. Thank whoever's in charge that it ain't you.

BLOODY SHOW: It's not what you hear when you are traveling through England: "Bloody good show!" In this case, the bloody show is the blood-tinged mucous resulting from the passage of the mucous plug. Go on, read that sentence again—I dare you (see Mucous Plug. Better yet, skip it altogether). The bloody show is often a classic sign of impending labor. However, like so many things related to pregnancy (see Due Date), you never really know when anything is actually happening. The bloody show can last for hours, days, or even weeks. It may be a classic sign of impending labor . . . or it might not. That being said—it is definitely freaking gross, but if you are lucky, you won't have to see it!

BLUE (and PINK): Boys wear blue. Girls wear pink. At least that's how it was in 1950. In today's day and age political correctness has taken over. Some parents will dress their boys in pink just to prove a point. Others might only use "neutral" colors like yellow or green. If you are going to avoid using blue or pink with your kid, you forfeit the right to get upset when someone refers to your newborn boy as "she."

BONDING: You will constantly hear about the importance of bonding with your new baby. Talk to her while she's still "in there." She will know your voice when she's born and this will help you to bond, blah, blah, blah. Stop right there. She will know your voice and what? Cry less? No. Wake up fewer times in the night? No. Soil fewer diapers? No. Bonding happens. It's natural, though not always instantaneous (see Postpartum Despression). Actually, it's much like what you do or used to do with your buddies on a golf course (see Golf). Regardless of how much you try, your kid will bond with you when he wants to bond with you. And, conversely, he won't when he doesn't want to. The same goes for you and your partner.

BOOKS, CHILDREN'S: You will read to your newborn. As a matter of fact, you may even read to her when she's a blastocyst, an embryo, a fetus, and then a newborn. And you will be doing this for the rest of your life, for even when they can already read themselves, they will always enjoy the sound of your tired voice trying to coax them into sleep. There are millions of children's books, but you will most likely be given the same ones that have been passed down for years. There's a chance that you will soon memorize some of these famous titles, such as *The Very Hungry Caterpillar*, *Goodnight Moon*, *Runaway Bunny*, *Pat the Bunny*, *Jamberry*, *The Cat and the Hat*, and *Curious George*, just to name a few. You will likely be struck by two salient facts. First, a lot of these seem to be poorly hidden pleas to get your kid to go to sleep. Second, some of these books seem tremendously old-fashioned. *Goodnight Moon*, for example is a cross between a children's book and the Steve Martin movie, *The Jerk*. Read it. You'll see. ("*Good night, table. Good night, lamp. Good night belly button lint.*") As a result, you'll swear that you could write a better book. But you can't. Besides, you won't ever have the time to actually do it, but just thinking you could write it might be all you need to get you through.

BOOKS: *The Girlfriends' Guide to Pregnancy*. The publications and resources that are available to pregnant women are mind-boggling. Walk into any bookstore and there are shelves and shelves of great information for soon-to-be moms. For dads? Not so much (see Invisible). The end-all, be-all expectant mom Bible, however, is Vickie Iovine's *The Girlfriends' Guide to Pregnancy*. Ms. Iovine has created a cottage industry of Girlfriends' Guides, and every woman will read these books. The fact is her book is hilariously entertaining, and you'll get bonus points for reading it. You sensitive guy, you.

BOPPY®/NURSING PILLOW: The Boppy® is a brand name for a nursing pillow (see My Brest Friend). A nursing pillow fits around your partner's stomach and supports the kid while he's nursing (leaving you somewhere between envy and reminiscing—so you think). You might also think of laughing since your partner may look funny walking around the house topless with the nursing pillow around her. Advice: Don't.

BOTTLE-FEEDING: At some point, the kid is going to need to get fed with a bottle. These bottle feedings may involve breast milk or formula or both, but the kid will need to suffer the indignation of sucking on a plastic nipple as opposed to the real thing (see Nipple Confusion). Bottle-feeding is actually a great opportunity for new dads to bond with their new kids (see Mannary Glands). Like a dog, at this stage, the kid just wants to go where the food is. So, if Dad can prove to be a solid provider of said nourishment—let the bonding begin.

BOTULISM: See Honey

BOUNCY SEAT: The bouncy seat is a must-have, must-register-for item. It's not so much that every newborn needs one—it's that every new parent needs one. This is how the math works: Kid cries = put kid in bouncy seat = kid bounces = kid stops crying. Whatever steps you can take to transition from "kid cries" to "kid stops crying" more quickly need to be taken seriously (since the more obvious and less politically correct means involving duct tape and wine are not likely an option your partner will go for). The bouncy seat is one of those tools that can speed up that process (see DVD: *The Happiest Baby on the Block*). After listening to your kid cry for (conservatively speaking) an hour or two—bouncing him in the seat is not only good for the kid, but also therapeutic for you! It's even encouraged by professionals with degrees (see Dr. Harvey Karp)! The kid sleeps. You feel better. It's a win-win!

BREASTFEEDING: Though men might think it looks fun, breastfeeding is much like baby-making sex. It's an extremely technical and scientific process that requires specialists (see Lactation Consultants), all kinds of equipment (see Breast Pump, Nipple Shield) and has a lexicon all its own (see Colostrum, Letdown Reflex). Truthfully, breastfeeding can often be a painful, complicated, emotional, and difficult process for your partner (still sound fun?). Many women have reported that breastfeeding was more difficult than their pregnancies, as breastfeeding is a time-consuming, exhausting process that may leave women with cracked, infected, and even bleeding nipples. Men, on the other hand, have complained of jealous feelings, as breastfeeding forges the bond between their new offspring and their partners.

However, just as men are happy not to be biologically equipped for childbirth, when the reality of breastfeeding is under-stood—men are equally pleased not to produce any milk (see Bottle- Feeding, Formula). On the other hand, if you are the type of guy who wants to experience everything his partner does, as authentically as possible, someone did invent this sort of inflat-able, fake-boob contraption that the non-breastfeeding partner or adoptive mother can wear around the neck, into which formula or breast milk is inserted, and the baby can suck to get milk out of (see Mannary Glands).

BREASTFEEDING, IN PUBLIC: There are few soapboxes in this book, but here's one: The kid needs to eat. Your partner's breast is food. Deal with it. Just know that some guy is lurking in the corner trying to get an eyeful of her breasts. Sick bastard.

BREAST MILK: Go on. Don't be such a wimp. Try it. Doctors say that it's the best nutrition for your kid's first months of life. And if breast milk alone can keep a kid alive for six months or longer, don't you really think you ought to know what this biological Kool-Aid® is all about?

BREAST PUMP: There are hand pumps and electric pumps. Again, sorry, the hand pump does not refer to your hand (see Breasts, Off Limits). The purpose of the pump is to... well, pump milk into a bottle. This helps alleviate the pressure of the full breasts (see Breasts, Engorged). The mechanical/electric breast pump is a scary looking device. It's huge. Your partner is hooked up to this machine that has tubes connecting to cups that fit over her breasts. The cups can be inserted into a specially designed bra to allow for hands-free pumping, which look like some sort of costume Madonna might wear on stage. You won't know whether to be petrified or amused as the milk is pumped from the nipples. But, if you get a look at your partner's tremendously distended nipples during this process—you'll know the answer.

BREASTS, ENGORGED: When your partner's boobs are full of milk, they are engorged (and can be relieved by feeding, pumping, or expressing). As fabulous as you might think they look (depending on your partner's physical traits—the whole boob-growing phenom can be awesome!), they are causing her great pain. And, as funny as you think it might be when these engorged boobs leak milk—don't mention it to her under penalty of death. Unless, you are out in public and you remembered to pack her an extra shirt in the baby's diaper bag (see Egg Shells, Hormones). One old wives' tale remedy that seemed to work well for us during my partner's first experience with engorgement was white cabbage leaves. Yes, you read right, white cabbage, not to be confused with red (really, purple) cabbage. You take the leaves off, put them in the refrigerator, and when engorgement first happens, you place the cold leaves inside the nursing bra. Call it strange as much as you want, but the deep, gutteral, relieved sigh your partner will utter when she inserts them into her bra will remind you of why you got into this mess in the first place.

BREASTS, OFF LIMITS AND SORE: Remember those fabulous nights when you were perhaps feeling a bit amorous and would play with your partner's boobs? Keep remembering that, cuz they're all you've got: memories. For the most part, those boobs may very well become off limits to you. Besides being sore and full of milk, there are potential breastfeeding issues that will keep your breastfeeling efforts at bay. And, frankly, your partner may not be feeling so hot about her own body and would rather you just played with your own boobs. There really is no telling when you'll have the opportunity to make your acquaintance with them again (see Sex, After Baby Making).

BREATHING: As in: Don't forget to keep (breathing). More importantly, don't forget the techniques that you will learn in your baby classes (see Lamaze). Oh wait, never mind, you'll forget those as soon as your partner goes into labor. The whole "he, he, he, he, he," thing goes out the window as soon as you hear or see the splash of broken water on the kitchen floor (or as soon as you hear any sentence that includes the words, "mucous plug" slip from your partner's lips). So, yes, simply don't forget to keep breathing.

BREECH: In that wonderful, perfect delivery world, the head comes first. In the not so perfect world, the kid wants to come out butt first. This is a breech delivery. When a fetus "presents"

as breech, doctors can attempt to turn the baby with
If the kid can't be turned, your partner will be whisk
to the operating room for a C-section.

BURP CLOTH: The burp cloth is something like a pocketknife
for new and expectant dads. It has so many practical uses. The
most obvious is to place it over your shoulder when you are
burping your baby after feeding. The reason for the cloth is that
your kid, when being burped, will likely spit up or throw up on
your shoulder. So, the burp cloth provides protection for your
shirt. After awhile, you'll simply stop wearing clean clothes and
it won't matter if the kid spits up on you. The burp cloth can
also be used as an impromptu changing pad, a cover for discreet
breastfeeding, napkin, magic prop ("Where's baby? There she
is!"), and primal scream muffler (your scream, not the kid's).

BURPING: This is another of those things you will learn in
baby class, but it's also likely something that you are moderately
familiar with just from being around other babies, new parents,
or your best friends since sixth grade. Everyone knows that you
have to burp the baby after he eats. He needs help getting the gas
bubbles out of his system. So after he eats, over the shoulder he
goes (or one of the other three or four ways that are acceptable).
For guys, the whole burping thing is great fun. On the whole,
we've always thought getting away with burping was funny (see
Gas, Wife), but now it's actually encouraged!

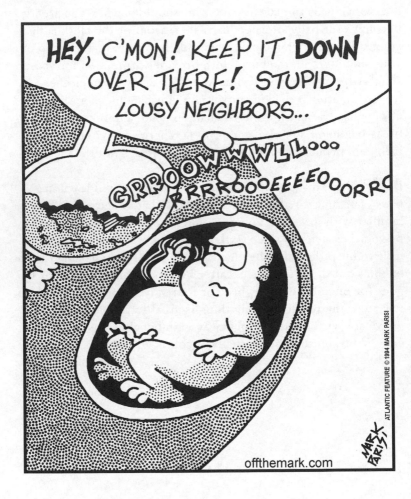

CAESARIAN (C-Section): Some babies are born via a C-section, which is a procedure that involves surgically removing the baby from the uterus. There is some honor in being born this way, as Julius Caesar was born via C-section. Though, it was probably called something different at that point, since there was no Caesar before Caesar. Although this is major surgery that requires a longer hospital stay, many men secretly harbor thoughts of their wife having a C-section versus giving birth vaginally for obvious reasons (see Episiotomy, Vaginal Rejuvenation). Many women—even those that don't experience any of the complications that might lead to a C-section— also explore the option of an elective C-section. During labor, if a doctor decides that a C-section is the best course of action, the ensuing managed chaos is impressive. Within 30 minutes in the operating room, you'll find yourself a new dad.

CALL LIST: Your partner has just delivered the kid. She's healthy. The kid is healthy. You're probably a little woozy, but otherwise doing okay. What now? That's right—you're expected to call the friends and relatives that have been driving you absolutely crazy for the last two weeks (or in the case of some family members—for as long as you've been alive) and let them know all the details that if they were patient, they could get in the mail (see Announcements). The call list is not to be taken lightly. If you leave someone off of this list, it's a slight that is not easily overlooked. And, if a family member finds out after another and feels that he should have been higher up on the list … well, suffice to say, it's a big headache. Work on the call list early on in the pregnancy. Consider it a "work in progress" and use it as a motivational tool to get what you want from friends and family, "If you don't back off—I'm going to move you down the call list and Dan will find out about the birth before you do!"

CAR SEAT: The car seat is perhaps the most important purchase you'll make prior to the birth of your child. And, it's also one of the most difficult. There are hundreds of options to choose from, and it's not like you have the option to sit in each of them to test them yourself for comfort and safety. This is where your partner's keen research within the built-in Mommy Network will pay dividends. Yes, *Consumer Reports* and other reviews will factor into your buying decision, but ultimately—it's all about your partner's friends. What do they have? What do they recommend? What fabric holds up the best, and, most importantly, accessorizes the interior of her car? Your kid will spend a tremendous amount of time in that first car seat, and you will spend a tremendous amount of time carrying the kid around in that first car seat. It's equal parts bed, transportation device, and throne. When you install the car seat in your car (not as complicated as some would make you think), you will automatically start driving 5–10 miles an hour slower, even if the kid's not in the car. And few things make you feel like Dad as much as seeing a car seat in your rearview mirror.

CARPAL TUNNEL SYNDROME: Not just for bad posture and the wrong desk height at work anymore. Carpal Tunnel is big in the newborn world. You and your partner will experience it from holding the baby incorrectly, feeding the kid at the wrong angle, and just generally being too exhausted to remember to do anything the way you used to.

CARS: During the pregnancy, your car(s) will no doubt become a topic of conversation. Do you have the right cars? Do you need to get a minivan? Should you get rid of the sports car and replace it with a sedan? Is your car safe enough? Is it easy to get the car seat in and out? Can you fit two strollers in the back? The thought of a minivan is enough to make some men consider calling an attorney and filing for divorce. After a few trips (see Baby Gear, Pack 'n Play™, Traveling), however, the minivan starts to look pretty good.

CHANGING PAD: When you first change the kid, you will always try to change her diaper on a changing pad. This is simply a soft, foam (or other material) pad that you put the kid on for her comfort. Usually it sits on top of the Changing Table (and there are portable pads that will travel with you in your diaper bag). After a couple of months, however, you'll change the kid on cold floors, rugs, couches, towels, lawns, back seats of cars, your knees, your lap, and just about anywhere else. It becomes something of a challenge to change the kid quickly in any environment. Would your dog stand still long enough for a diaper change, including 14 wipes? Try it. There's your answer.

CHANGING TABLE: Yet another piece of furniture that you need to purchase for the baby's room (see Crib, Glider). After all, you need something to put the changing pad on! The changing table is where you'll likely store your diapers and other required diaper changing gear. It's the command center for the war against dirty diapers.

CHECKING OUT OF HOSPITAL: Depending on whether your kid was born vaginally or via C-section, you will spend between one and five days in the hospital. Frankly, with a full-time staff of trained medical professionals at your (more or less) beck and call, there's a chance you won't want to go home. But at some point you do need to check out. Prior to leaving the hospital, the nurses will run you through a checklist of information. They will make sure you have a proper car seat (some hospitals will not discharge the baby without a car seat). They will make you sign the birth certificate that will assign your child his or her legal name, for better or worse, for the rest of its life. You will likely see the nurse's lips moving, but not hear a word. You'll wonder what that deafening thumping sound is and realize it's your heart trying to leap out of your chest. And as you walk to the exit, the nurses will give you a smile that is a mix of excitement for you and huge amounts of empathy. You just KNOW that the second you're out of earshot, they all start laughing, "Poor bastard. He's screwed." This is it. When you step out of those doors, you are a parent (see Hell Night, Night Nurse).

CIRCUMCISION: If you've had a girl you can skip this one. If you have a boy, you'll have to give thought to whether or not to circumcise the little tyke. Religious beliefs aside—the decision to circumcise the kid is simply this: Personal. Some people do it. Some parents choose not to. There are arguments about "looking like his daddy." There are arguments about cleanliness. Whatever. The right answer is the one that you and your partner agree on. It's not like you can ask the kid. Isn't it obvious what his answer would be? "You want to do what with that blade? Where? Oh no you don't!"

COLIC: Tell anyone that your kid has colic and you'll get the same reaction: a sympathetic, pained look with a gentle head nod, which says, "Holy moly, you're screwed." Colic is a condition that in the most simplified terms means your kid cries for hours and hours and hours—in a row. Day after day. Night after night. True, all newborns will cry day after day, night after night, but colicky babies cry more. Colic does attack one in 10 babies (or is it the parents that it attacks?), and doctors don't know exactly why it happens (see DVD: *Happiest Baby on the Block*). Often times, colic is caused by abdominal pain. At first you feel really bad for your baby, as he is obviously unhappy and uncomfortable. After the third or fourth hour, however, you may feel worse for yourself.

COLOSTRUM: Before your partner starts producing breast milk (if applicable), there is this gooey, sticky yellowish substance (Stop it! Right now! Grow up!) that is packed with nutrients for the baby and secreted from the breasts. You don't want to be trying this particular substance. After a couple of days, the colostrum will go away and the kid will get pure breast milk.

COMPETITION: The whole "my kid is better than your kid" thing starts early. The competition among pregnant women or new moms is intense, as they "discuss" how hard and how often their babies are kicking, how much milk they produce, their APGAR Scores, how soon the kid sleeps through the night, and on and on. In sports, baseball is thought to have the most detailed, asinine statistics, but parenthood may take the big prize. The percentiles, growth charts, and more make for a less-than healthy competition among parents. It starts early—and probably never ends.

CONCEPTION: There is no turning back.

CONEHEAD: (see Hole in the Head). Do not be alarmed. If your kid is born vaginally, his head is going to be a bit misshapen, or a lot misshapen (see Fontanel). He's going to look like a conehead. The birth canal is not a huge, wide passageway. And in order to get through this passageway, the head is going to take a few lumps. The plates of a baby's skull are not fully formed or fused and won't be for a couple of years. So as he slides through, the head gets misshapen. It's normal. And, it's funny looking. That's what they make those cute little caps for. Deal with it.

CONSTIPATION: Your partner will have it. You'll hear about it (see Breasts, Sore; Hemorrhoids). One word: Colace—ask your pediatrician or OB/Gyn if it's okay for her to take. This laxative is available over the counter, does not function like a bomb, and comes in a small gel caplet.

CONTRACEPTION: True, it's not needed during the pregnancy. However, there is a completely false rumor that if your partner is breastfeeding or has not yet gotten her period again, she cannot get pregnant. Wrong! Do you really want children 10 months apart? No glove, no love. Let it be your new mantra until you are ready to add to your family again.

CONTRACTIONS: When the contractions start, the panic starts. Your partner's abdomen will tighten as the muscles (say it with me): con-tract. The contractions will feel different to different women: Some experience a cramp-like feeling, others feel their bellies harden, some feel intense back pain, and some feel nothing at all. Despite your desire to get the car started and race to the hospital, it's not yet time. The friendly medical staff at the hospital has no interest in seeing you until the contractions occur at regular, predictable intervals (every five minutes) and last for one minute—for a full hour like clockwork. Get a stopwatch, pen, and paper handy. You'll never need your basic math and recording skills more than at this moment.

CONTRACTIONS, BRAXTON-HICKS: As if you're not freaked out enough by the fact that your life is about to change drastically and forever—your partner may very well experience Braxton-Hicks contractions, otherwise known as false labor. These contractions, which often occur following heavy activity, have the potential to send both you and your wife into panic mode. And they can go on for months before your due date. Depending on your partner's level of paranoia and how much she reads baby-related Web sites, Braxton-Hicks contractions can cause you as much pain as they do her.

COOING: There's not really a testosterone-driven way to write about cooing. It's just the greatest sound you'll ever hear and a reward for enduring all the sleepless nights, early morning feedings and blow-out clean ups. Your baby will just look up at you and make the most gentle, cute little sound you've ever heard. And, it'll melt your heart. Now … go change a tire, pound a nail, or get greasy or something.

COOLER, THERMAL: Though not Operation Overlord, serious planning and preparation goes into getting ready for the delivery of a baby—where to deliver, doctor selection, and what to do with your faithful dog. Though much emphasis (and rightly so) is placed on the mother-to-be and the unborn child and what she needs to pack to make her stay as comfortable as possible, let us take a moment to consider the well-being of the father/partner during the delivery process. The actual delivery can occur many hours from when you arrive at the hospital. You are going to get hungry. Though many hospitals provide food and snacks, it makes sense for you to be prepared, on this day of all days, by packing a cooler filled with your favorite treats to take with you to the hospital. Here are some helpful hints to consider when packing The Cooler:

- There is no stopping on the way to the hospital. Women in labor will not look kindly on a quick stop to your favorite deli, no matter how good the sandwiches are!
- Consider ready-to-eat items that can be consumed quickly. The expectant mother may go hours unable to eat or drink, so be discreet.
- Avoid items that need to be refrigerated, even if you have ice packs or dry ice at your disposal. Anything fresh sitting in a cooler for 36 hours cannot remain pristine enough to eat. Unless, of course, you eat the fresh stuff right away. But we're betting you won't have much of an appetite early on in the process.
- Though some hospitals allow beer, alcohol is for after the baby is born, not before.
- Other items to consider include breath mints or strips.

CORD BLOOD: Umbilical cord blood holds stem cells. Stem cells have the unique ability to adapt into other cells and stimulate new, healthy growth among specific cells throughout the body. This is all technical stuff that means that if your child ever has one of the diseases that stem cells can treat, you are ahead of the game because you have a clean source to access the stem cells specific to your child's DNA. In a perfect world, your child will never need to use those stem cells (for bone marrow transplant, to treat leukemia, to repair heart tissue, etc.), but it's something you should talk over with your partner and doctor.

COT: If you went to camp as a kid, you probably had to sleep on a cot from time to time. Assuming you stay in the hospital with your wife (see C-Section, Vaginal Delivery), you will long for those camp cots. The hospital cot is the absolute bottom of the bedding food chain. It's fraud to call that plastic-whatever a mattress, and the squeaks of the springs rival the most piercing sound you've ever heard—and not in a good way. If you have a bad back, neck, knee, or temperament when you are hurting, schedule a visit to the chiropractor or masseuse, in advance, for after you leave the hospital. Not like you're going to be able to make that appointment or any other that has to do with your personal well-being for the next four months, but it doesn't hurt to give it the old college try.

COUVADES SYNDROME: If you feel the need to give yourself a fancy French word for something simple (see Bassinette, Layette), tell people that you have Couvades Syndrome. In actuality, Couvades Syndrome is simply what is known as sympathy weight (see Opportunity Weight). Couvades is the French word for "lazy soon-to-be-father who uses his partner's pregnancy as an excuse to pack on extra pounds." The French can really stuff a tremendous amount of meaning into one word. A study at the University of Wisconsin–Madison found that two species of male monkeys also gained weight when their mates were pregnant. Ain't evolution grand?

CRACKED NIPPLES: At any time, should you think that breastfeeding is fun, have your partner show you her cracked, dry, bleeding nipples. Cracked nipples are just one of any number of lovely afflictions your breastfeeding partner may suffer (see Mastitis, Thrush).

CRADLE CAP: Your baby comes out perfect. Then a few weeks or a month later he develops this scaly redness on his head. Sometimes the redness can also occur in the creases of his neck and armpits and behind his ears. No, he is not turning into an iguana. When this occurs on the scalp, it's called cradle cap and it's very common. No one knows exactly why this happens, but hormones, yet again, are primary suspects. Regardless, I know that when I told my mom about it on our kid, she told me that she just scrubbed the bejeesus outta my head and then lubed it up until it went away. This is yet another prime example of why you don't ask your own parents for advice. Call the pediatrician.

CRAVINGS: You've heard the stories of the soon-to-be dad who makes midnight runs to the local convenience store to pick up a specific flavor of ice cream? And when he gets home, he's sent off again to get some obscure flavor of jelly and a stick of beef jerky? It happens. The cravings come fast and furious. What's most curious is that your vegetarian partner will suddenly crave and devour all kinds of meat (see Hormones). Or it's been years since she ordered dessert after dinner and now all she wants to eat is pie (see Couvades Syndrome, Opportunity Weight). There aren't any scientific certainties explaining why the cravings occur. Of course, there are very few scientific certainties explaining why pregnant women do most of the things they do (see Egg Shells, Hormones).

CRIB: Another piece of freaking expensive baby furniture (see Baby's Room)? You betcha! This one, of course, may actually be necessary. The kid does need somewhere to sleep. And he does need to be somewhat caged, as you don't really want him rolling out of bed and falling to the floor. What isn't necessary, most likely, is spending more on the crib than you did on your king-sized mattress and bed frame. Parents spend so much money on things that the kid won't even remember or use (see Toys). You can amortize the cost of your crib purchase, however, as many cribs will transition to "the first bed" when the kid is old enough.

CROWNING: For some of these words, the visual is all that is really necessary. No need to be overly flip or sarcastic. Here's one of those times. Crowning is when the baby's head starts to peek through your partner's vagina. It's when the head starts to come out. The question is: Are you even looking there (see High or Low)?

CRYING, BABY: You may think that changing diapers will be your worst nightmare, but your baby's cries are truly the worst thing you can imagine. There should be entire books devoted to learning how to handle the cries. But the fact is that the only way to deal with the crying is to just deal with the crying. Consider it your sentence for rolling your eyes at crying babies on planes over the years. It's your turn. The reality is that crying babies aren't so bad in daylight. However, that exact same cry at 3:00 A.M. is brutal! And, when it goes on for hours (see Colic) and night after night (see Sleep Deprivation), it certainly takes its toll. New parenthood is a study in patience and perseverance. The crying is frustrating, since you know something is wrong. Despite the fact that you are convinced your kid is the smartest baby ever born (see Competition), you just can't figure out what he's crying about! He's eaten. He's burped. You've changed his diaper. He's warm enough. Go to sleep! You just have to know that the crying eventually stops, and when it does you are rewarded (see Cooing). Eventually.

CRYING, WIFE OR PARTNER: Unlike the crying baby, who cries because something is wrong, your wife will cry because everything is right. Or she'll cry because the stoplight didn't change fast enough. Or because her food is cold. Or because the baby is cute. Or because the sky is blue. Pregnancy wreaks havoc on hormones. Having a baby isn't a picnic—it's major bodily trauma. The physical and emotional rollercoaster is intense and completely unpredictable. Your mission (and you have no choice, but to accept it) is to be the rock of stability and support. The hormonal imbalance may last weeks, months, or longer (see Postpartum Depression), but be strong and you'll get through it all … together.

CUTTING THE CORD: There are literal and symbolic factors at play with the cutting of the umbilical cord (see C-section, Vaginal Delivery). Your baby is entering the world and you are welcoming her in with this hugely important act. When you cut that cord, she goes from being totally dependent on your partner to also being dependent on you (see Bottle-Feeding). Don't worry, calm your nerves, it doesn't hurt the kid! As you cut that cord, you are also severing any ties to your old life. It's gone. You are a dad now. A parent. It's no longer just about you. The transition happens instantly.

CVS: (see Amniocentesis). Chorionic Villus Sampling (CVS) is an alternative, less-common procedure to Amniocentesis, during which the sample is taken from the placenta instead of the amniotic fluid. Where amnio is often performed around 15 weeks, the CVS test can be done as early as eight weeks, for those who really want to know the gender of their baby and know that the baby is healthy as quickly as possible (see Baby's Room). Like an amnio, the CVS test is performed with an impossibly long needle, but unlike the amnio, the needle is usually inserted through your partner's cervix. Don't look. Really. Don't.

DAD/ FATHER: What you will be. Wow. Holy cow.

DATE NIGHT: The days of "Hey, honey, feel like Chinese tonight? Want to go to Chef Chu's?" spontaneity ended when you cut the cord (see Cutting the Cord). You'll be so busy with changing diapers, making bottles, and trying desperately to get even four minutes of uninterrupted sleep that you won't have time to go out with your partner. As a result, it's important to schedule time together. Yes, you have to actually schedule the time. So now it's: "Hey, honey, let's go to Chef Chu's a week from Thursday. Do you think your parents will watch the baby? No? That's their bridge night? Okay, then what about your sister/my sister/my brother/anyone?" Not as romantic and spontaneous, but at least you'll get some Chinese food— and time alone with your partner.

DIAPER: How can something that seems so harmless be so ... not harmless? In reality, the diaper is your friend. The diaper keeps a big mess from being a much, much bigger mess. There are all kinds of diapers from which to choose: cloth, disposable, environmentally friendly, branded, licensed, and more (see Baby Gear). Like every issue related to pregnancy there are always two (or more sides) about the "right" choice. The left will tell you that the cloth diapers are more environmentally sound. The right might say that cloth diapers end up using more natural resources (e.g., water) to clean. Frankly, you should really only have one consideration when choosing the right diaper for you and your baby: Which one works? If you feel guilty about using disposable diapers, but know they are a better option for you, just buy a hybrid car. Then you'll be even.

ATLANTIC FEATURE © 1994 MARK PARISI   offthemark.com

WAIT...
THAT CAN'T
BE RIGHT...

THE NEW FATHER STRUGGLES
WITH DISPOSABLE DIAPERS.

DIAPER BAG: There are few things that zap your manliness faster than throwing a diaper bag over your shoulder. They aren't made with you in mind (see Invisible). You will quickly get over any self-consciousness when you realize how versatile the diaper bag is. It carries everything you would need to take care of your kid when away from base camp (see Baby Gear, Burp Cloth, Changing Pad, Diaper, Flask [for you], Formula, and Wipes). You may be able to negotiate with your partner and have a say in the diaper bag that she purchases. Men have designed attempts at the "daddy diaper bag," but there really isn't any way to make it cool.

DIAPER PAIL: What do you do with those dirty diapers when they are changed? Put them in a diaper pail. That's the easy part. It's when you have to open the diaper pail to take out a full bag of dirty diapers—now that can get the slightest bit gamey. But, like all things about daddyhood, you'll get used to it. At least, you better, since you'll be changing between 10 and 12 diapers a day at the beginning!

DIAPER RASH: No, this isn't something that happens to you from changing too many diapers. It's a common affliction that babies get. You know that chafing you get when you wear a wet bathing suit for too long? That's about it. But with your baby all you have to do is slap on a little ointment and it will usually clear right up (sort of like that rash you had in college, but didn't tell anyone about). If it does not clear up or if it starts to bleed or look really angry, call the pediatrician. To help avoid diaper rash you can air-dry your baby and also make sure you change diapers frequently.

DIAPERS, CLOTH: One diaper option. There are services that pick up dirty cloth diapers and deliver clean ones. The price for this monthly service ends up being about the same as using disposable diapers. The instructors of baby classes like to make fun of the dads' inability to actually use cloth diapers.

DIAPERS, DIRTY: Prospective dads hate the idea of changing diapers (see Meconium Poop). You can expect to change your new kid's diapers somewhere between 10 and 12 times a day at the beginning. The early days are "easy," as the poop (that's the technical term you will learn in the hospital) of babies fed by breast milk doesn't really smell. However, because breast milk acts as a laxative, there is quite a bit of poop—smell or no smell. At first, new dads, mortally afraid of any leakage, may take as long as five minutes to get one diaper changed. Rest assured, however, that once you get used to it, you treat the changing of a diaper like a NASCAR pit stop. And changing diapers becomes as much a part of the day as brushing your teeth, showering, and getting dressed. New dads with boys have extra challenges (see Baby, Pee-pee TeePee™, Penis, Spraying).

DIAPERS, DISPOSABLE: The quickest and easiest way to change diapers. You change the diapers and throw out the dirty ones. If you're out and about, no need to hang on to the dirty diapers and bring them home. Just toss them in the trash can. Finito!

DIET/NUTRITION: There's a good chance that whatever diet you and your partner followed before the pregnancy quickly went out the window with the pregnancy (see Cravings, Sympathy Weight). Your partner will be told all about what to eat and what not to eat (for the sake of the baby), and the chances are good that you'll become hypersensitive and overreact—thereby, turning yourself into the food police (see Alcohol, Cravings). This is not a good idea. A solid rule of thumb is this: Let your partner eat whatever she wants to eat. Her body is being ravaged. You, on the other hand, need to watch what you eat or you'll end up as big as she is.

DILATION: On its own, dilation just means enlargement, stretching, or expanding. If you've ever had a comprehensive eye exam, you've probably had your eyes dilated. This isn't that. This is the measurement that doctors use to determine whether or not "it's time." When the cervix is dilated 10 centimeters, it's time for your partner to start pushing (see Birth Canal, Conehead, Fontanel). Spread your fingers apart 10 centimeters. Your kid is gonna squeeze through that—or not (see C-Section). There's a chance that your partner's water will have broken already, you'll race to the hospital, and they'll still send you both home because she's "only four centimeters" dilated. You may be told to walk around the halls of the hospital, since exercise and gravity can really help speed along the dilation process (see Walking the Halls).

DIRECTIONS, READING: With fatherhood comes the responsibility to put together tons of toys and furniture (see Baby's Room, Batteries, Nursery). There are many different contraptions (see Baby Gear) from swings to bouncy seats to rocking horses (or rocking Harleys). As you may find yourself assembling many of these items at once, you might actually want to—this is difficult for me to say out loud, too—read the directions for each item. While this may break a number of Man Laws, the fact is you are going to be tired and following the directions keeps these activities somewhat mindless. If you follow the directions, you'll only have to put the item together once (as opposed to pulling it apart and starting over when you realize that the second piece is in backward). Once your kid is old enough—you can go back to putting together his toys without the directions (and get your Man Card back).

DOCTOR'S APPOINTMENTS: There are lots of 'em. Do you need to go? That's up to you and your partner. They are actually pretty cool. It's amazing when you hear the heartbeat for the first time (and a huge relief). Of course, you need to get your ultrasound pictures. These are your first baby pictures and though it's nearly impossible to make out the difference between a head and a foot, your family will go on and on about how cute she is (see Competition). It can get a little crazy, "Did you see the ultrasound? Is that the best ultrasound picture you've ever seen? What do you think the over/under is on her APGAR score will be? She's an eight at least." After a while, the doctor's appointments get a little mundane until the last few. Then you have the one at which you get to hear the Holy Words "Any day now" (see Due Date).

DOULA: There's a good chance that while you may have at least heard most of the words in this book, but didn't know what they meant, the term doula remains totally foreign. The doula is a person (usually a woman) who assists in the birth and delivery of the baby and is sometimes referred to as a midwife. Yes, in theory, that's what you are, but some women opt for the comfort of an experienced coach in the labor room. Perhaps in terms you'll better understand: If your partner is The Team and the doctor is the head coach, the doula might be your partner's personal trainer. You, on the other hand, are the water and towel boy.

DR. HARVEY KARP: As close to a god walking on Earth as you will find. If you ever see him walking the streets, bow to him and avert your eyes. Every new and expecting parent should be required to watch *The Happiest Baby on the Block*—a DVD that delivers magical results. Dr. Karp performs some sort of baby voodoo. Don't ask questions, just revel in the results. In fact, if you don't have the DVD—put this book down and go get it. Now! Go!

DRIVING: (see Cars, Car Seat). Being a dad immediately knocks a minimum of 5–10 miles off your average speed. You pay far more attention to the road (and maybe even put your cell phone down). God help you, however, if the kid starts hollering for food when you're alone in the car without the food source nearby.

DUE DATE: A myth. A fraud. The due date is traditionally 40 weeks from conception (note: 40 weeks is actually 10 months!). The date is set by your partner's obstetrician/gynecologist (OB/Gyn), based on the size of the baby at the time of the first appointment. It means nothing. The vast majority of babies are considered "full term" and can be delivered without any worries at 37 weeks. Or they can be a week late (note: Many first-time mothers are late). Take comfort in the fact that most doctors will not allow a pregnancy to exceed 41 weeks. Once expectant mothers reach 37 weeks, the waiting period until delivery is nothing short of torture. Once you reach the due date, friends, relatives, and people you barely even know will start calling (every day) to find out your partner's status. To avoid these daily calls, the second after conception has been medically confirmed, smart expectant fathers might consider scheming with their partners to create a due date that's a few weeks beyond the actual date. That way, when the little tyke actually arrives, you can deal with the well wishers at your leisure (see Announcements, Call List).

EATING, BABY: When the kid is born, she needs to eat every two or three hours, all day and night. A feeding officially starts three hours after the beginning of the last feeding (not from the end of the last feeding). The mistake that is often made is assuming that after the kid eats, she sleeps. Early on, it may take an hour to feed the kid (see Bottle-Feeding, Breastfeeding, Mannary Glands) and another hour to get her to go to back to sleep. So this means that you will have exactly one hour to sleep before the next feeding (see Sleep Deprivation). This pattern goes on for weeks and weeks— until you'll slowly start to cut out the middle of the night feedings and four uninterrupted hours of sleep becomes reason to celebrate.

EATING, PARENTS: It seems like you never eat and when you do—it's fast and standing up (see Diet/Nutrition). You might get out for a meal with your new kid and when you do—you'll feel like a rock star. When the kid is only a few weeks old, it's actually pretty easy to go out to restaurants because the rumble and motion of the vehicle you use to get there usually knocks out the cranky little tyke within minutes (see Car Seat).

ECLAMPSIA: Toxic complications that can occur late in pregnancy involving symptoms such as headache, vertigo, visual disturbances, vomiting, hypertension, edema, convulsions, and/or coma. This is a serious medical condition (see Pre-Eclampsia).

ECTOPIC PREGNANCY: The medical terms are much less fun to learn about. An ectopic pregnancy is pregnancy that is not in the uterus. It's basically what happens when the embryo settles and grows in any location other than the inner lining of the uterus. Most ectopic pregnancies occur in one of the two fallopian tubes. However, they can occur in other locations, such as the ovary, cervix, and abdominal cavity. They must be surgically removed or they can cause the tube to rupture, leading to internal hemorrhaging, and even death. Ectopic pregnancies are considered medical emergencies.

EDEMA: The medical explanation for why your partner is sporting "cankles" (loosely defined as cow ankles). After waddling around all day (likely in the "pregnant woman power position" with her hands supporting her back), water is retained in her legs and particularly her feet and ankles. So they swell. Remember, she's not exactly comfortable. Refrain from making fun of her. Do not sing the "This Little Piggy" nursery rhyme to her; it ain't funny. And after the delivery, if she has been given a medicine called Pitocin to speed up the labor, there is a possibility that those cankles will look like twigs compared to what Pitocin causes—good news is that the edema soon goes away.

EFFACEMENT: As your partner's body prepares for birth her cervix thins. This thinning is called effacement. The doctor will measure the effacement in percentages (e.g., 50% effacement, 75% effacement, etc.). At 100% effacement, the cervix is in the best position for birth, as dilation will occur more easily (see Dilation). Okay, let's try this again—the higher percentage the effacement, the more likely your kid is finally coming. Better?

EGG SHELLS: Nothing to do with breakfast, brunch, or those cute art projects you did in elementary school. Egg Shells is what you'll be walking on for the better part of 40 weeks during the pregnancy—and for the foreseeable future after the kid is born. Your partner's hormones are as unpredictable and as potentially ferocious as Mount St. Helens, and you want to take special care not to cause any eruptions. Walk softly. Carry no stick. And, understand that there are likely no battles worth picking during this time. Remember: She looks beautiful pregnant and under no circumstances does her behind look like it's getting bigger.

EMBOLISM: The E words are loaded with medical jargon. An embolism is a blockage of a blood vessel by a foreign substance or a clot. An amniotic fluid embolism is a rare condition that can occur during childbirth. This is a serious medical condition.

ENGORGEMENT: See Breasts, Engorged

EPIDURAL: After enduring the discomfort of pregnancy for 40 weeks (see Due Date), it's only fair that your partner be given the opportunity to load up on the drug cocktail that is the epidural. Women have been known to want to write songs about the epidural. Basically, an anesthetic is injected directly into the epidural space surrounding the fluid-filled sac around the spine. If it works just right, the result is that your partner is feeling no pain and her abdomen and legs are numbed. There are potential complications to epidurals and some women even opt to have a "natural childbirth" (see Natural Birth) free of any drugs or painkillers. They believe that whatever pain they feel is part of the experience and they do not want to be denied any of the experience. The women who do receive the epidural think these other women are insane.

EPISIOTOMY: It's safe to say that most men don't really want to know about the episiotomy. Okay, here goes: Sometimes the baby is too big for the vaginal opening and a surgical cut is required to increase the size of the opening to allow more room for the baby. While horrible sounding, the alternative is vaginal tearing. Following the birth, the doctors will stitch up the cut. Best to avoid the temptation of asking the doctor in front of your partner if she can "just add a couple of extra stitches" (see Egg Shells, Vaginal Rejuvenation).

EXERCISE: It's important for your partner to exercise and stay fit during the pregnancy. This might include hiking, walking, and even jogging up to a certain point. If you are a fitness buff, you might find your regular routine interrupted and your workouts shortened (see Golf, Sympathy Weight).

EXPENSES: Many couples choose not to have kids because they think that they need to be better prepared financially. Perhaps not a bad decision. Pregnancy and the kids are expensive propositions. Beyond all the stuff you have to buy, you end up buying more stuff that you don't really need (see Baby's Room). Plus, babies grow like weeds, so their clothing only fits for about a week before you need new clothes. Baby clothes can be inexpensive but not when you're buying new stuff every week. And with diapers and food (while it's okay if the kid wears a shirt that's too small—it's traditionally frowned upon to skimp on the healthful meals and clean diapers), you can quickly rack up some serious monthly expenses. Don't even get started on what the hospital stay is going to set you back (see Insurance).

F

FALSE LABOR: See Contractions, Braxton-Hicks

FAMILY: All kidding aside, it's pretty cool that you have a kid. Pretty cool that you're now a dad. Your partner is a mom. Together, you are all a family! Your new immediate family. That you chose, not the insane people you were saddled with at birth. Families are really great. Good luck (see Fear).

FEAR: Holy moly, you have a kid! What the heck were you thinking? When in doubt about how to conquer this feeling of panic and fear, the best bet is to always go with your gut. The good news is that the parenting instinct kicks in somewhere around the time that you cut the cord. It's as if one switch shuts off (the "let's go grab a beer" switch) and another simultaneously flips on (the "she's just tired" switch). You'll be fine. No. Really.

FEEDINGS: See Eating, Baby: Food, In Food Out

FENUGREEK: (see Breastfeeding). Once again, the scientists are stumped as to why something happens, but the natural herb, fenugreek, is said to stimulate and increase a mother's milk supply. Plus, it will make your partner smell like maple syrup. There are special teas called Mother's Milk and others that she can drink while breastfeeding. Check beforehand with your pediatrician regarding this and any other herbal concoctions you might be considering because they can sometimes cause stomach upset in the baby or interact with other substances.

FERTILITY CLINIC: You're reading this book, so you are expecting a baby. How you got here could have happened in a variety of ways. Some couples seem to get pregnant by looking at each other from across the room. Others need a bit more help, and that's where the fertility clinic comes in. There are all kinds of tests, poking, prodding, hormone treatments, shots, dissolving caplets inserted in the vagina, and tests for you and your sperm. Some people get lucky enough to have someone else carry their child for them. If you are one of these people, it means that even though you've had to go through hell and back to get your baby, that your partner can get in her skinny jeans the day the baby lands in her arms (see Infertility, Secondary Infertility)!

FINGERS AND TOES: Right around the 20th week, your partner will have an important ultrasound taken. This is the one where the fingers and toes are counted. There's this moment of trepidation, but once you count all 10 fingers and all 10 toes—that anxiety becomes relief and cause for celebration (see Doctor's Appointments).

FONTANEL: See Hole in the Head

FOOD INTOLERANCES: See Allergies

FOOD IN, FOOD OUT: (see Diapers, Feedings, Poop, Seedy Yellow Poop). During the first few weeks of life, it seems like every time the baby feeds, the baby immediately poops. Welcome to Infant Reality 101. And stock up on the diapers.

FORCEPS: Giant medical salad tongs that a doctor might use to turn the kid the right direction or even pull her out if she's starting her life a little stubbornly. Forceps don't seem to be used as much as they used to, so many OB/GYNs instead take them home to use as barbecuing tools.

FORGETFULNESS: Sleep deprivation leads to brain malfunction. Being a new parent makes you stupid. It's a fact. You won't be able to find the sunglasses on your head or the keys in your hand. You're lucky to remember where you put the kid. This will continue until your kid starts sleeping through the night— regularly sleeping through the night. If, for example, it takes your kid three months to start sleeping through the night, it will take you another three months to recover and for your brain to catch back up. Some mothers insist that you will permanently lose one-quarter of your brain's memory capacity per child. So if you have four kids total, well, you do the math (see Pregnesia).

FORMULA: Doctors nowadays endorse breastfeeding whenever feasible because of the nutritional benefits to the baby and the bonding effect breastfeeding has for most mothers. Many mothers endorse breastfeeding because once you get the hang of it, it's so much simpler than mixing and shaking and heating and sterilizing bottles. Plus, they can't ever forget their breasts at home. Sometimes, however, new moms don't produce enough milk and the baby's food supply needs to be supplemented with formula. If this happens, there's a good chance your partner will feel guilty about this (see Crying, Wife), even though it's not her fault. Chances are the kid will eat whatever you give him (see Ounces). Plus, this gives you the opportunity to have special bonding time with the baby when you get to feed him in the middle of the night. Just what you wanted.

FREE TIME: Oh, please!

GAS, BABY: Your baby will fart and burp like a champ. And it's always funny. There's something about this tiny, little being with absolutely no control over its bodily functions ripping farts and burping as if he'd just downed a pint of Guinness in a pub competition. It gets even funnier when after a few months the first few smiles on the kid's face are the result of gas and not any kind of muscle control. Even just a few months old and babies think farts are funny. See! We were right for once: It's innate. Therefore, we can't help it.

GAS, WIFE: Depending on your partner, there's a chance that she hasn't ever farted or burped in front of you. Or there's that chance that she never stops burping and farting in front of you.

Pregnancy will either introduce or increase a level of gas production in your partner that you didn't think was possible. You'll wonder how in the world there could possibly be a gas shortage in the world when your house is constantly filled with it. You'll have to fight the urge to call your local gas company and ask them to make sure your home is safe. And never, ever light a match to find out yourself.

GENDER, FINDING OUT: To find out or not to find out, that is the question. This is another of those personal issues that only you and your partner can decide, but that everyone in your life feels they have the responsibility to weigh in on (see Breastfeeding, Diapers, Eating). If you find out, you can get started on buying all the items specifically needed for that gender (see Blue and Pink). If you don't find out, you and your partner will have this big surprise. Sure, you want a happy, healthy kid with all of his fingers and toes (preferably left-handed with a big, breaking curveball), but the truth is your reaction and mental preparation is completely different for the different genders. If you have a boy—you start thinking about when he starts dating with a smile. If you have a girl—you dread the mere thought of her dating. It takes preparation.

GESTATIONAL DIABETES: See Glucose Tolerance Test

GETTING SENT HOME: Your partner is in labor and you race to the hospital. You are completely prepared to get checked in and have the baby. And then they send you and your partner home. She might not be dilated enough. She might be having false labor. There are any number of reasons why they send you back home. But none of them are good enough. It's exhausting to race to the hospital with all that anticipation, adrenaline, and dread fueling your body. It's even worse to get sent back home. Since Murphy's Law always seems to work, be sure to leave your wife's suitcase and your cooler at home when you go to the hospital—that way you will ensure that she will get admitted (see Cooler).

GIFTS: Obviously, you will be given a huge number of gifts and presents (you have, after all, registered for them!). Of the 250 presents that you receive, you may actually use 10 of them every day. The worst part of the gifts is the never-ending exercise in writing thank-you notes. You haven't slept in weeks and you're getting calls from your family, "Did you ever get the thingymabob that I sent?" Gifts are also a pain because the stores pack anything with foam popcorn. You could get a bed sheet packed in Styrofoam. Then there are the boxes that need to get broken down and recycled. The gifts are nice, but they end up causing more work than enjoyment. Think ahead to gymnastics classes, baseball gear, confirmation, bar/bat mitzvahs, college, weddings, down payments on houses ... Register at your local bank. Ask for cash instead. You'll still have to write thank-you notes, but at least you'll be saving the environment.

GLIDER: It's just a freaking chair! (see Baby Gear, Baby's Room). But because it's marketed as a baby room product, the manufacturers have the opportunity to mark up the price by at least 100%. The glider is a chair that allows you to rock back and forth (or glide on rails) while you're holding and/or feeding the baby. Ideally, this movement makes the kid go to sleep. And, in theory, anything that makes the kid go to sleep is worth it. But, just call it a chair.

GLUCOSE TOLERANCE TEST: Otherwise known as a glucose challenge test (GCT) or a glucose screen, this test is usually given to the mom between 24–28 weeks of pregnancy to check for gestational diabetes. It won't give you a diagnosis, but it does indicate if your partner is one of the 2–7% of women who might need further testing or who might acquire gestational diabetes. What it means is that your pregnant partner, instead of just having to deal with hormones coursing through her body and making her like a Jekyll and Hyde, also has to control her blood sugar levels with strict diet and exercise. The good news is, the condition usually goes away after the baby is born. The bad news is that if you decide to jump in again and give your baby a sibling, your partner has higher risks of developing gestational diabetes in her pregnancy or later in life.

GOLF: Who are you kidding?

GRANDPARENTS (Relatives): There's that age-old saying that other people's kids are the best, because you can play with them and give them back (see Quotes & Clichés). Grandparents illustrate this saying perfectly. They will spoil the kid and give her all kinds of things that you might not want her to have. But since it's a special relationship that should be fostered, you cannot protest too loudly when they ply your kid with chocolate, cookies, and sweetened juice and then send them home for the evening (well, you can, but then they will just teach your kid how to sneak and lie). The flipside: Grandparents and other relatives are the best babysitters because they, too, adore your little bundle of joy.

GROCERY SHOPPING: Impossible. In the early days after delivery there really isn't any time to go grocery shopping. Any moment you have when the kid is sleeping, you will spend trying to sleep yourself, or trying to get the house straightened up. You will need to rely on your friends and relatives for food. You will become a hermit. And, it's okay. Enjoy it. Eventually, you will escape from the house again and when that happens, even foraging for food becomes somewhat of a guilty pleasure: Ahhhh, all those clean aisles, all that quiet, all those fresh vegetables that we'll never have time to stir fry in wine again ...

HAND SANITIZER/ HAND WASHING: There's nothing that will make you think about washing your hands more often than having a new kid. Because he is susceptible to all kinds of germs, and because there is nothing worse than a sick baby, you will find yourself carrying around little tubes of hand sanitizer and placing them all over your house. You won't even let anyone who has not doused their hands in the stuff or washed their hands in hot water and soap three times over hold your kid. It becomes a bit of an addiction, and you'll put the hand sanitizer on your hands constantly. Grabbing the steering wheel? Need some hand sanitizer. Picking up a pen? Need some hand sanitizer. Just back from the restroom where you washed your hands for 10 minutes under scalding hot water? That's not enough. Get the hand sanitizer! If you're not careful, you will end up asking people to wear some sterile gloves before picking up your kid. Hmmm, now there's a thought.

HEARTBEAT: There's an amazing moment that comes when you hear your baby's heartbeat for the first time. As you leave the doctor's office, you and your partner will share a private glance and smile. When you are alone—you will remember that heartbeat and smile. You may even learn to do a pretty cool imitation of it which sounds like a cross between Darth Vader's asthmatic breathing and galloping horses. And then it will hit you: A heartbeat means your life is totally about to change (see Fear).

HEATING PAD: If you don't have one, get one. For you and all your soon-to-be aching parts.

HELL NIGHT: The first night home from the hospital. If your partner had a "regular" vaginal delivery (what's so regular about that?), she will probably spend two nights in the hospital. If she has a Caesarian (see C-Section), she will spend four to five nights in the hospital. During this time, you have access to a full staff of nurses and doctors, and the kid will likely sleep in the nursery. When you leave the hospital, the nurses and doctors don't come home with you, and the first night alone with your new "little miracle" can be a long, sleepless night of hell. With no call buttons to push, it's now up to you to change the dirty diapers at 3:00 A.M. (see Meconium Poop) and find a way to get him to go back to sleep after his feedings. Many times, your kid may fall asleep just before it's time for his next feeding. For some new fathers, "Hell Night" is reported to be the longest night of their lives. Bad news, sometimes hell night morphs into hell week, hell month —it's the luck of the draw.

HEMORRHOIDS: Your wife may get them. Not you. Just another reason to celebrate the fact that you aren't the pregnant one. Privately. Celebrate privately.

HICCUPS: Your baby will get the hiccups while she's still "in there." Early on, your partner will just tell you about it, but later in the pregnancy, you'll actually be able to see the kid moving with each hiccup. Talk about alien invasions! Wow.

HIGH CHAIR: (see Pets). As a brand-new parent, you won't have to worry about the high chair for a while. That's not to say that you shouldn't register for it and have someone buy it for you. You just won't need to use it. When you do, you will discover that it will be a pain to clean three-plus times a day and the seating pad starts to smell weirdly fungal after a while. And you won't learn till your second kid that one of those reclining seats that you can strap on to your kitchen chair and then toss into the sink works just as well. Finally, the best thing about not using an actual high chair is that you have one less huge, primary colored, baby object invading your space.

HIGH OR LOW: The position you will take in the delivery room when it is time for your partner to start pushing. "High" refers to staying up around her shoulders, holding her hand, stroking her hair, and feeding her ice chips. "Low" refers to being "down there" holding a leg, and pretty much getting a glimpse of the whole ball game in all its glory. If you're really brave, they might even let you "catch" your baby (but it's not likely, since the baby-dropping rates among new dads do not make for impressive hospital-safety stats). Your choice may change when you see the videos in the baby classes. There is no shame in staying high (see Baby Class).

HIGH-RISK PREGNANCY: Generally, any woman with a chronic illness and/or who is over age 35 and/or who gets pregnant with multiples is considered a high-risk pregnancy. Only about 5–10% of pregnancies are termed high-risk. And of those who get the diagnosis, 90–95% of those pregnancies produce healthy, viable babies. In other words, it's a term designed to scare the bejeesus out of you, even though for the majority of women it probably means nothing besides maybe some bed rest later on in the pregnancy.

HOBBIES: You may have had one or two before your kid came along. You don't anymore (see Golf).

HOLE IN THE HEAD: When your baby is born you might notice that it seems to have a hole in its head. This soft spot on the top of the skull is called a fontanel. The truth is that your kid has six holes in its head, but the big one on top is the one we are talking about here. This soft spot is another example of the amazing design of the human body. The loose connections of the skullbones that intersect in the soft spots make labor and delivery possible. Without this flexible anatomy, either babies would have to have smaller brains or mothers would have to have wider

hips. This spot is covered with a tough membrane and while you should not poke at it, it will go away when the baby's skull bones fuse together.

HOME BIRTH: Not even going to tell you what it is, because you shouldn't even consider it. Not to be judgmental, but what's wrong with you? And who do you think is going to have to clean all that up after the delivery? Not your partner. Think about it.

HONEY: No, we're not talking about the pet nicknames you and your partner saddle each other with for life. We are talking here about bee honey. Because there's a slight risk to your baby of developing infant botulism, it is generally recommended that babies not be given bee honey during the first year of their life.

HORMONES: When the pregnancy hormones kick in, they really kick in. A friend had an experience with pregnancy hormones that still makes me shiver. Here it is. In his words: "I'm still not sure what confluence of biochemical reactions and interstellar events came together when my wife was seven months pregnant. She was going through the normal and expected reactions to the hormones surging through her mind and body. She experienced heavy mood swings. She was cranky, constantly in nesting mode, and suffering from various other mental, emotional, and physical maladies (see Egg Shells). I had somewhat learned how to deal with my wife's out-of-nowhere crying, screaming, and weirdly violent outbursts. But what followed during the seventh month was so unexpected and shocking that the results actually ended up being broadcast on *Dateline NBC* (no joke). What was so horrible? What was so scandalous that it made national TV? Well. What my wife wanted, more than anything else in the whole wide world … at that moment … in her hormonally challenged state of mind … was for the two of us … to make a video and lipsync to the Backstreet Boys. Yup, the Backstreet Boys. Oh, it gets better. Her inspiration for all this madness was a video spoof made by two Chinese students, who by the way don't even speak English. So she wanted us to make a video spoof of the video spoof? Yeah, I still don't get it. So let my experience be both an example and a warning to you. DO NOT, I REPEAT, DO NOT let your pregnant, hormonally challenged partner get any goofy ideas when you have easy access to a camcorder, a broadband Internet connection, and a YouTube.com account. *Dateline NBC* picked it up and soon everyone in the universe had access to my most deeply felt humiliation."

Poor Michael. On the other hand, some women in their second and early third trimester get so horny, so full of desire, that all they want to do is have sex. Sounds too good to be true, but it hasn't yet shown up on one of those urban legend Web sites, so it could really be true somewhere, with some women, right?

HOSPITAL, ROUTE TO: You have seen the TV shows and movies where the husband frantically, erratically races to the hospital? It may or may not be like that, but you should definitely know the best route to the hospital based on traffic patterns.

Come on, you're a guy! Practice driving to the hospital, but don't tell your partner—she'll probably mock you mercilessly, making your trusty, innate, usually infallible male navigation device go dead at the precise moment the water breaks (see Batteries). You need to know every possible way to get your partner from your house to the hospital in the shortest possible amount of time. Once labor starts, your goal is to get her in the hands of those that know what they are doing. Everything you "learned" in the baby classes will be forgotten once labor begins. You also want her to get the epidural as quickly as she can. If your partner wants drugs, of course.

HOSPITAL, TOUR: Prior to "the big day," you and your partner will take a tour of the hospital. This tour is supposed to provide you with a comfort level for what will happen when you come back in to have your kid. You'll see a birthing room, recovery room, the nursery, and the juice machine from which you will pour yourself and your partner huge cranberry, orange, lemonade concoctions during your stay. Be warned: There will be one person on your tour who has read everything there is to read about the hospital experience and this person will ask endless questions. When you come back to check in for real, there will be staff there to assist you. You won't and don't need to remember everything! Just remember how to get to the hospital. And if you have the option to pre-register, do that. You probably don't want to be filling out forms while your partner screams bloody murder if you can avoid it.

HUMIDIFIER: Get a cool-mist humidifier—it's a lifesaver if your kid has a stuffy nose. Chances are that she will. And chances are that the purring hum of the motor will also calm her down.

HURL: As in "I think I'm gonna." Birth is not for the weak. If you are averse to blood, intimate body parts, and seeing your partner stretched open by an object the size of an adult bowling ball, then you might want to watch a series of graphic horror films prior to the delivery. Consider it training. Besides your own hurling, there are ample other opportunities for vomiting during and after pregnancy (see Blow-Out, Hyperemesis, Morning Sickness, Spit-Up).

HYPEREMESIS: One in 300 women is afflicted with hyperemesis, which is a condition of excessive vomiting during pregnancy. That's the bad news. The good news? Hyperemesis usually stops on its own and has no negative effects on the baby. Ten percent of women get hyperemesis with uncontrollable, violent, projectile vomiting that, if it does not stop, can result in a hospital stay to rehydrate the pregnant person. If your wife is one of that 10%, you might think twice about giving her the aforementioned "good news" about it not usually having a negative effect on the baby. She's not likely to care as she launches her breakfast across the room.

HYPOCHONDRIA: Sometimes it's better to have no information rather than too much. Since your partner is experiencing so many new physical and emotional sensations, she may find herself researching these feelings on Web sites like BabyCenter.com. In doing so, she may also convince herself that she's that one in a trillion women afflicted with a rare condition. Never mind that the only way to contract this condition is to climb one specific tree in the southeastern region of Zimbabwe while chanting an ancient Swahili prayer recently translated from Biblical Aramaic. And never mind that your partner has never been to Zimbabwe, much less Nebraska. She's convinced that she's got it (see Hormones). Have her call her previously pregnant friend (guaranteed that she has one). Her friend will talk her down from the tree (in English).

ICE CHIPS: Any other time during your life, ice chips are simply … chips of ice. In a delivery room, however, they are the only "food"/liquid your partner is allowed to eat or drink. To help her keep from getting dehydrated, you will be feeding her ice chips throughout the entire labor. Keep in mind that these are her ice chips and though you might think of taking one or two for yourself, best not to do that with her watching.

INCOMPETENT CERVIX: While the terminology actually sounds sorta funny, "Dude, you are such an incompetent cervix," there is nothing funny going on here. If the cervix dilates abnormally, it will be impossible for the uterus to hold the fetus in, which can result in a miscarriage.

INCONTINENCE: Usually reserved for the elderly and those Depend® commercials, incontinence is basically peeing on yourself when you don't want to. Pregnant women and new mothers, however, sometimes get this condition as a little bonus. It's bad enough that their nipples might be ripped up, stretched, or leaking milk, and now this? This is just another reason that you know why women think that all men are lying when they say, "If I could be pregnant, honey, I'd do that for you." They are right. It's all lies, lies, lies (see Kegels).

INDUCING: Sometimes your doctor will recommend that you induce labor, or, in other words, make the little bugger come out when you want it to not when it decides to. The decision to induce is made as a result of many different factors, but is usually recommended for the safety of the baby, your partner, or both.

INFERTILITY: This refers to the persistent inability to conceive a child. Sometimes the doctors can figure out why and fix it. Sometimes they cannot (see Fertility Clinic). Since you're reading this book, we'll assume that you've got the conceiving part down now (see Secondary Infertility).

IN-LAWS: Chances are you have your own definitions and special terms for your in-laws and don't need any help from this book.

INSURANCE, HEALTH: Having a baby is an expensive proposition (see Expenses). It's crucial that you have good insurance coverage for the hospital visit. If you so much as look at some piece of equipment, there's a good chance you'll get charged. And you need to do that before you get pregnant, because once you do, the insurance companies can refer to your pregnancy as a "pre-existing condition" and refuse to cover it (Nice, huh?). So it's important to have some level of insurance coverage to offset the charges. Getting the hospital bill in the mail is not a happy day even with good coverage.

INSURANCE, LIFE: When you're a strapping young lad, you don't give much thought to the whole life insurance thing. But when you have this tiny, defenseless being that depends on you for everything—you might want to call Ned (Ned just seems like an appropriate "insurance guy" name. Like Ned Ryerson from the movie *Groundhog Day*).

INTERNET: The Internet is teeming with information about pregnancy. Your partner will likely scour sites high and low in search of pregnancy facts and figures, not to mention the random thoughts of strangers. Which, until this day, she might have ignored, but now have somehow morphed into her own form of gospel (see Hypochondria).

INVISIBLE: As a soon-to-be dad—it's what you are. The 40 weeks of pregnancy are not about you. Your job was done when the line showed up on the stick. It's time to duck back into the shadows and let the attention be heaped on your partner. When it is time for someone to talk to you, you will likely be asked something like, "Are you taking care of [insert your partner's name here]?" Go check out *Parenting* magazine. It's not for you. *Child* magazine? Nope. Now, if there were one called, *Donor News* … that might have some content for you. Even a checklist of "must have items" offered by Babies "R" Us includes a heading entitled, "Just For Mom." The items under this heading include: pictures, frames, film, and videos. After all, why would a dad be interested in such things?

iPOD: The labor process can take hours upon hours and hours upon hours. It can take days. So it's important to have some music in the birth room. Bring your iPod—loaded with all kinds of different types of music for the different parts of the birth experience (labor, recovery, etc.). You will not be able plug the iPod into the wall in the delivery room, so bring lots of batteries and speakers, too.

IT IS WHAT IT IS: You may not subscribe to this philosophy prior to parenthood, but you'd best start practicing now. It is what it is is a simple way to explain the things that you simply just don't understand (and never will). "How do you deal with cleaning up all that poop every day?" your friends will ask. "Dude, it is what it is."

JEALOUSY: You are gonna feel it. You'll be jealous of your kid. You'll be jealous of your partner. You'll be jealous of your friends that don't have kids. You'll be jealous of the 18-year-old kid down the street with the hot girlfriend. This entire experience is really about your partner (see Invisible). So just deal with the fact that you will be on the sidelines quite a bit. And for quite a while.

JUMPER: A toy that you'll wish you could use. A couple of bungee cords hang from the ceiling, or a doorway, and attach to a seat. Your kid sits in it (once he can sit up unassisted) with his legs dangling out and his feet touching the floor. It's great for him because as soon as he starts to jump up and down, he'll screech in glee. It's great for you because the jumper keeps him entertained. Another win-win, man!

KEGELS: Oh come on … you know exactly what the Kegel muscles are, don't you? If not, you are missing something good. Kegel muscles are the ones that grab the inner parts of a woman's pubic area tighter so that she can control her bladder, urinary flow, etc. These muscles have specific exercises developed by Dr. Arnold Kegel (imagine the research he had to do to identify the muscles and then come up with the exercises used to strengthen and tone that area!). Kegel exercises restore muscle tone and strength after pregnancy (see Incontinence).

KICKING: Once the kid starts moving around, you and your partner will be able to feel her kick. The strength and frequency of the kicking is a pretty good indication of her personality—or so they say (see Advice, Unsolicited, They). If she's just moving all over the place and kicking like a member of the U.S. Women's National Soccer Team, there's a good chance you've got an active little girl on your hands. As the due date gets closer, you may actually see her feet and hands as she kicks and moves around. It's like a scene right out of *Alien*.

LITTLE RACHEL IS SHOWING STEADY WEIGHT GAIN, GOOD MUSCLE STRENGTH, ABOVE-AVERAGE COORDINATION, AND A PHENOMENAL SPITTING-UP DISTANCE...

MARK PARISI ATLANTIC FEATURE © 1994 MARK PARISI offthemark.com

LA LECHE LEAGUE INTERNATIONAL: An international organization whose mission is to "help mothers worldwide to breastfeed through mother-to-mother support, encouragement, information, and education and to promote a better understanding of breastfeeding as an important element in the healthy development of the baby and mother." In reality, the LLLI is like an army that will stop at nothing in an effort to enforce breastfeeding. Yes, it's proven that breastfeeding is indeed better for the baby and fosters better health. LLLI is not for the faint of heart, but they mean well. As always—you do what's best for you and your partner.

LABOR: Getting that baby out is work. And that's why it's called labor. Here's a big surprise—you and your partner won't know when it's going to start or why. And sometimes it doesn't start on its own at all (see Inducing). Signs that labor has started include the passing of the mucous plug and regular, sustained contractions (see Contractions), effacement and dilation of the cervix (all words you know by now if you're reading this A through Z), and the water breaking. Some of this may occur in the hospital and some of it may lead to the mad dash to the hospital (see Hospital, Route To).

LABOR PLAN: When labor starts everything you've read and learned goes right out the window. Remember how you'd study for a test and when the instructor put the exam on your desk, your brain went completely blank? That's what this is like; only instead of failing history, you're failing life. No pressure, dude. And that's because you have a labor plan filed with the hospital. This includes your pre-registration information, as well as instructions for the nurses and doctors. Informative comments from your partner like, "Get that f*ing epidural in my spine as quickly as possible." If you are familiar with the labor plan, you will be far less likely to experience your partner auditioning for the lead female role in a remake of *Carrie*.

LACTATION CONSULTANT: The lactation consultant's job is to help your partner learn how to properly breastfeed your new baby. The consultant may also be someone who helps your partner cope with the fact that she is struggling with breastfeeding or helps treat cracked nipples, etc. In many cases, she is on your partner's side and wants to help her succeed in a way that is comfortable for everyone. Your partner might want to research and create a relationship with a lactation consultant prior to the birth of the kid. If there are any breastfeeding challenges that come up, don't wait to seek professional help. Have your partner talk to a lactation consultant immediately.

LAMAZE®: One of a number of birth class philosophies and options. While Lamaze is a brand name and philosophy, like Kleenex, Xerox, and TiVo, it's become the umbrella term for baby classes (see Baby Classes).

LATCH: When the kid is properly positioned on your partner's nipple and the milk is flowing, it is said to be a good latch.

Creating the right latch is equal parts physics, geometry, fine motor skills (your partner's), prayer, and luck.

LAYETTE: What is it with the French names and having a kid (see Bassinette, Couvades Syndrome)? Layette is just an expensive name for "stuff your newborn baby needs." Layette consists of onesies, T-shirts, receiving blankets, swaddling blankets, towels, washcloths, socks, hats, burp cloths, and sleepwear. So why is there a need for this term? Why can't you just go out and buy these things individually? Because if it didn't have a fancy name, they couldn't charge more (see Expenses).

LEAVING THE HOUSE: Unless you have a premature baby or a child with challenges, you'll be ready to leave the house with your kid after a couple of weeks of 24/7 confinement. By now the fear of whether or not you can handle it will have subsided a little. Plus you'll be completely stir crazy. The first time you leave, you will either overpack the diaper bag so grotesquely that you have to swap it out for a rolling suitcase, or you will forget everything except the kid. Both are acceptable and understandable. If you are heading to a restaurant, go somewhere that you know (and might even be recognized). You want to be surrounded by friendly faces (but not friendly hands—remember the germ thing?). Or at least go to one of those places that you know is totally kid friendly, but until now you've avoided like the plague. Keep going out. It gets easier. And before long, you will time your outings with her naps and she'll sleep through the entire meal (see Car Seat).

LENGTH: Not about you. This is one of the key facts that will forever be tied to your kid. And it will be immortalized on the baby announcements. The length and weight of your kid provide endless opportunity for intra-grandparent comparisons (see Competition). "Ashton was 19 inches? Oh. Hmmm. Well, Genny was 23 inches." Yes, but Genny's parents are both well over 6 feet tall and she's likely to be ridiculed when she's 7 feet tall at age12. Not sure she's going to like that too much.

LETDOWN REFLEX: Try to follow this: In order for your baby to actually breastfeed, milk must flow. The letdown reflex allows the milk to flow. The letdown reflex is equal parts physical and emotional response. If your partner is stressed, chances are the letdown reflex and therefore, breastfeeding, will fail. As a result, it's important for your partner (if she wants to breastfeed) to do so in a relaxed setting. The letdown reflex can be triggered by your baby crying or when your partner's body knows "it's time" to feed. Physiologically, this signals a part of the brain to release oxytocin into the bloodstream. When it reaches its target, the milk-producing cells contract and the baby eats. And when it's eating, it cannot cry—well, not really.

LEUCORRHEA: A condition that results in a white discharge coming out of your partner's vagina, often a sign of infection. It doesn't happen to you.

M

MANNARY GLANDS: These are made for the partner whose breasts are not producing the milk so that he or she can experience what it feels like to breastfeed. What they are missing out of the experience (besides authenticity) is the 60 or so pounds of pressure a baby's tiny mouth can exert on the nipples. Yes, that's right. More pressure than is in your tires, dude. Mannary Glands are like this big glove-like contraption ... just go rent *Meet the Fockers II*. Robert DeNiro's character wears these while feeding the baby to avoid nipple confusion. A bottle fits into the artificial breasts. Just give the kid the bottle. And if you must use the Mannary Glands—don't let your friends see you wearing them. Ever. Chances are you will never live it down.

MASSAGE: You will need to give your partner daily (if not more) massages. Her lower back, legs, feet, and shoulders are going to take a beating during and after the pregnancy. You will do it.

MASTITIS: Mastitis is an infection of the breast that usually only occurs when women are breastfeeding their babies. Think you're a "breast man"? You're nothing compared to the baby who is now latched on to your partner's nipples at every possibly opportunity. Mastitis occurs when, due to the force of the suckling, the nipples get sore, cracked, or scratched. This creates a small opening through which bacteria can enter. Bacteria combined with the sugary nutritional content of breast milk can multiply until they are plentiful enough to cause an infection in the breast (see Thrush). It only happens in about 2% of breastfeeding women, and it usually happens more than two to four weeks after delivery. It hurts, it requires antibiotics, and it's not fun.

MATERNITY CLOTHES: Repeat this phrase, "Honey, you look awesome in that outfit." Maternity clothes have fortunately come a long way and are now far more stylish than they used to be. But if your partner asked you if she "looks fat in these jeans" before she got pregnant, rest assured she's going to ask both during and after the pregnancy. The proper answer, regardless of the fact that she may look like a well-dressed model who just happened to swallow an entire basketball team, is: "Honey, you look awesome in that outfit." Repeat after me: "Honey, you look awesome in that outfit."

MECONIUM POOP: While some babies actually lose this poop while still in the womb or during delivery, most babies save it for their arrival. Meconium poop is sterile and odorless, but it's the stickiest, blackest, most tarlike substance you will ever see coming from your baby's newborn butt. It even bubbles on exit. Yeah, it's pretty gross. And a lot of dads get to deal with it because their partners are kinda out of it after delivery. But if you're still in the hospital, you can fake stupidity and get a nurse to handle the clean-up. If not, prepare to use about 17 wipes to scrape it off that poor little baby's newborn butt. And it gets even more interesting (see Seedy Yellow Poop).

MIDWIVES: See Doula

MISCARRIAGES: (see Incompetent Cervix, Secondary Infertility). A miscarriage or spontaneous abortion is a pregnancy loss that happens before the 20th week of pregnancy. After the 20th week, the loss is called a stillbirth. Miscarriages are an unfortunate reality that strike 15–20% of all pregnancies. That number goes up as a woman ages. Miscarriages happen for all sorts of sad reasons. And no matter how many times someone tells your partner and you that it was for the better, you are still going to feel as if you lost your baby. Because you did. If the grief gets to be too much to handle alone, seek professional help.

MOBILES: Another item that you will register for (see Baby Gear, Batteries). You'll have mobiles over the crib, over the Pack 'n Play™, and maybe even over the changing table. They range from simple to complex (with lights, music, and multiple D batteries). As soon as the baby can stand, you should consider removing the mobiles because the kid can pull on them and bonk his soft, little head.

MONITORS, BABY: There are a variety of baby monitors from which to choose. There are monitors that only broadcast sound. And then there are the Big Brother ones with sound and live video feed. Early on, if your child is asleep in another room, you will likely be obsessed (to the point of mental illness) with every sound and movement that she makes. Or if she's too still or too quiet, you'll be driven equally insane. Watching and listening to your kid will become an addiction, but is potentially good practice for when she is a teenager and has a boy in the house. An imaginary boyfriend, of course. Real ones will not be allowed near your daughter until she is 35.

MONITORS, FETAL: This strap-on device around the womb allows your doctor to check the baby's heart rate for stress during pregnancy, labor, and childbirth. You can buy cheap-o fetal monitors, but most doctors discourage self-monitoring of any kind because every time the baby shifts in the womb, making the heartbeat hard to discern, pregnant women start breaking down their doors at all hours of the day and night. If you are under 35 years of age, and pregnant with a singleton, you will likely only see a fetal monitor during your hospital stay. All the older women with multiples, however, become more familiar with this device early on.

MOOD SWINGS: (see Hormones). Duck and take cover. The mood swings can come quickly and without warning. And, there's nothing you can or should do. Take the body blows and move on. If you feel the urge to defend yourself or fight back, count to whatever number you have to in order to make that urge go away. You will not win any battle that results from a mood swing. And there are no situations where you will be allowed to be right or to win. Give it up. Give in. Let it go. This too shall pass (see It Is What It Is).

MORNING SICKNESS: Morning sickness is the blanket term explaining why your partner is hurling. Most women think that a man made this term up because real morning sickness, when it hits hard, is a 24/7 deal. Some women puke. Some women just walk around for months feeling like they are on a sinking ship during a hurricane in the Bermuda Triangle of pregnancy hell wishing they could puke. It's bad. There's nothing you can really take for it. And eating works to take it away, but only while she is chewing; it comes back the second she swallows (see Opportunity Weight). So-called morning sickness primarily occurs during the first trimester (see Hurl), but for some women, it may last longer. The good news is that for many women, they wake up one day and it's gone. Small miracles …

MORPHINE: Your partner may be offered morphine, the be-all and end-all of all pain medications, to help ease her pain during the initial contractions, but before she's fully dilated. If she turns it down, you might try to get some for yourself.

MUCOUS PLUG: Perhaps one of the most gross terms in the English language. The mucous plug is like a cork that protects the cervix against bad stuff. As the cervix starts to dilate, the plug can come out in one fell swoop or in stages. While it is common for labor to begin with the expulsion of the mucous plug (see Bloody Show), the mucous plug can also come out over time. Mucous plug. Say it out loud. It's just gross, right? Mucous, as a word on its own is bad enough, but "mucous plug"?

MULTIPLE BIRTHS: Congratulations! You're having twins, triplets, quads, whatever. Anything more than one qualifies as a multiple (see Singleton). One newborn is hard enough. More than one (see Fear, Expenses, Morphine?)

MY BREST FRIEND™: A special circular pillow to help prop the baby during breastfeeding (see Boppy, Breastfeeding).

NAMES: Naming your kid is a huge decision. With the wrong name, you may sentence your child to a series of playground beatings that will last for years (Richard Balls, or Harold Coque, for example). There are all kinds of influences that factor into finding the right name (or eliminating the wrong ones!): Family, ex-partners, favorite celebrities, songs, poems, childhood experiences, former pet names, and more. You can find tons of books that list the most popular baby names. Books that list every conceivable baby name. Books that list the meanings of different names and the various international translations of that name. And just as many Web sites do the same thing. The easiest way to determine the right name is to ask your parents and in-laws which name they prefer. Just kidding.

NANNY: See Au Pair, Babysitters

NARCOTICS: (see Morphine). Often given in the early stages of labor to ease the pain (your partner's pain). If doctors had a penny for every new dad that asked, "Can I get some, too?" they'd be very, very rich. Don't try to be funny. They've really heard it all.

NATURAL BIRTH: Natural birth is simply described as a vaginal delivery without any drugs (see Epidural). How is putting a body through all that trauma without any help considered "natural"?

NESTING: Nesting is this amazing instinctual ritual that overtakes women just before the baby is due. It's just like it sounds, only instead of flying around like a bird to collect branches and leaves to create a nest for a new little chick, very pregnant women waddle around (their hands always on their hips or lower backs) and collect furniture, paint chips, (even more) baby clothes and credit card debt while creating the perfect nest for their own new little chicks. You will spend many days participating in the Nesting Triathlon—an event where you go to at least three stores in one day. Don't complain. In those waning days you end up with a new couch, new fireplace, new baby room, new entryway rug, and (best of all) a new flat screen TV. Not that you'll ever get to watch it (see Diapers, Egg Shells, Golf, Sleep). And, just before the kid comes home, there's this moment of nesting perfection. The house is done. It's clean. Everything is in its place. The nest is ready. There's sort of an inner peace for your wife. And then the water breaks.

NIGHT NURSE: In an effort to ease their way into parenthood (see Hell Night), many couples choose to hire a night nurse for the first few days, weeks, or longer. The night nurse comes to your house and assists with the night feedings in an effort to help you and your partner get as much rest as possible. Of course, they charge so much money that it hurts. Simply having an extra set of hands is all you might really need. You don't really need a professional nurse to bottle-feed a baby at three in the morning. But it's up to you. Correction: It's up to your partner (see Invisible).

NINE MONTHS: (see Due Date). In your brain, you're probably thinking nine months is nine months. Not so much. It's actually

40 weeks. And if the kid is "late," as can happen with first babies, you are really looking at closer to 10 months. It's better to just count the weeks.

NIPPLE CONFUSION: (see Bottle-Feeding, Breastfeeding, Pacifier). Sometimes babies who are fed exclusively from the breast for the first few months will reject the bottle. (And, really, who can blame the kid? He probably gets his mouth on the plastic or silicone nipple and is thinking, "What the hell? Something's just not right.") Conversely, some babies who get the bottle early might not feel comfortable on the breast—the breast is usually much more work for less milk per suck. The fact is that the breast and the bottle require different sucking skills. And sometimes it's too much for the little tyke to figure out which is which. So he gets confused. And he cries. And your partner cries. And you feel like crying, but you're a dude, so you can't just cry whenever you feel like it. Don't worry, if he gets hungry enough, he'll figure it out.

NIPPLE CREAM: (see Breastfeeding). Since the nipple can take such an intense beating during breastfeeding, lactation consultants will often suggest using a nipple cream and a nipple shield to help heal the damage.

NIPPLE SHIELD: The nipple shield is designed to help ease the damage done by breastfeeding.

NOISE MACHINE: This may look like an alarm clock, but instead of emitting horrible beeping noises, it emits soothing sounds like the ocean, a rainforest, a river, etc. Babies like white noise, so it works great for them. Just beware: Those sounds might make you have to pee all the time (see White Noise).

NON-STRESS TEST (NST): Late in the pregnancy, NST may be performed to test the baby's heart rate, movement, and heart rate "reaction" to movement (the heart rate should rise as the baby moves). It also tests the positioning of the placenta and can measure the amount of amniotic fluid. Many non-stress tests are performed if the due date has come and gone, and is used as a key influencer in the decision to induce labor. So the baby is late and

the doctor needs a test to determine if the baby is still "safe"—what the hell is so "non-stressful" about that?

NURSERY: After the baby is born, she will be placed in the nursery and monitored. You will have the option of keeping the baby in your room with you at all times, but you've got the rest of your life to be woken up in the middle of the night to address your children's needs. Your choice. If you're British or highly pretentious, you might use the word nursery to refer to the baby's room (see Baby's Room).

NURSES: Depending on the hospital and your length of stay, you will see a number of different nurses during your partner's recovery. While they are all working to ensure your partner's comfort and safety, they all have different beliefs and agendas (see Breast-feeding, La Leche League, "On a Scale of 1–10," Pacifier). Every eight hours the rotation will shift and you will need to learn the "baby beliefs" of your next nurse. As you get to know each nurse, however, do your best to charm each and every one—if you're good at it, they'll take care of all those first diaper changes (see Meconium Poop). As well, you can milk nurses (perhaps "milk" is the wrong word in this case) for information and free supplies.

NURSING BRA: Where the hell was this when you were dating or first married? A bra that allows her to just pop out the breast with no effort at all. Lift the shirt, lower the cover over the breast, and out pops the nipple. It's for the kid (see Jealousy).

OB/GYN: An Obstetrician/Gynecologist will be your partner's doctor during the pregnancy and delivery.

"ON A SCALE OF 1–10": (see Quotes and Clichés). Your partner will constantly be asked about her pain and what it is "on a scale of 1–10." She should always increase the pain number by at least one or two—just in case she gets a nurse that doesn't believe in pain medication (see Nurses).

ONESIE: (see Layette). A simple, single piece of clothing that snaps around the diaper. It's likely to be your baby's official uniform for the first couple of months.

OPERATING ROOM: If your partner needs an emergency C-section, she will be whisked to the OR. The flurry of surgeons, nurses, pediatricians, neonatologists, and anesthesiologists that participate in the dance to remove the baby is well choreographed and impressive! The time from the decision to go with a C-section to the baby being lifted out of the womb is about 30 minutes from start to finish.

OPPORTUNITY WEIGHT: (see Sympathy Weight). There's a good chance that you'll gain a few pounds during your partner's pregnancy (see Couvades Syndrome). The reality of any weight gain isn't that it's based on "sympathy" at all. It's opportunity. You see, prior to getting pregnant, there's a chance that your partner didn't like sweets (or any other specific foods that you love). Perhaps desserts weren't usually ordered. Maybe salads were the meal of choice. After your partner gets pregnant, she might start eating things that she normally wouldn't eat (see Cravings). Her cravings might include Pop-Tarts®, sourdough bread, pasta, mac and cheese, pork ribs (which she hadn't eaten in years), chocolate, and lots of meals at her favorite restaurants. So...it's your "opportunity"! You get to order whatever you want—and/or finish what she doesn't. It's great fun.

OUNCES: What you measure your newborn baby's food in (if fed formula or pumped breast milk). You will become obsessive about the number of ounces she drinks every day. And you will be impressed with how much more she eats from one week to the next. The problem is, you will never figure out how they calculate the ounces of breast milk that goes directly from nipple into baby's mouth. And if you are formula mixing, make sure to add the water first and then the powdered formula.

YOUR BLADDER: BABY'S FIRST SQUEEZE TOY.

PACIFIER: (see Nipple Confusion). As you've learned, there are usually two disparate camps for every topic related to pregnancy—the pacifier is no different. There are those who feel that the pacifier is a crutch that leads to bad teeth. In the other camp are those who feel that babies are oral and comfort themselves with sucking and that unless your partner wants a 7.5-pound, 24/7 boob ornament, pacifiers are good things. You will probably have at least one nurse at the hospital try to dissuade you from using it and who will border on scolding you if you do. Recent studies, however, have found that kids who use pacifiers to sleep have a lower risk of SIDS. Philosophical arguments aside—whatever gets your kid content, quiet, and to sleep can't be all that bad, can it?

PACK 'n PLAY™: The (Pack 'n Play) is a portable crib, play yard, and storage container. When you have the nerve to start traveling with your kid, you will bring your Pack 'n Play.

PAINT CHIPS/ COLORS: (see Nesting). You and your partner will likely redecorate and paint part, if not all, of the house in the months leading up to the birth. During this time, you will go to stores and check out the wide variety of paint colors available. Have fun with this and create a little game—your partner calls out a color name and you have to guess what color it actually is. What color is "Afternoon Siesta"? You can have fun for hours.

PAPERWORK: There's a lot of it. From your insurance to the hospital registration and labor plan, you will feel inundated with questionnaires. Get them done early.

PARENTING MAGAZINES: More like Mommy Magazines (see Invisible).

PARENTS: A label that you will never shake. It's what you and your partner will become. It defines you. You may find your entire personality shifting and surprise yourself by starting sentences with "When you become a parent…" as you explain to your childless friends why you are no longer any fun. If you catch yourself doing this, try this little exercise: Go say it to a mirror. See how silly you look and sound? Becoming a parent means your life changes. It doesn't mean you die!

PASSIVE AGGRESSIVENESS: With pregnancy, your partner's senses are heightened. Her ability to smell a plate full of macaroni and cheese that's being served 10 miles away is mind-boggling. You, on the other hand, will become quite adept at filtering out all of the passive aggressive comments that will be thrown at you from all sides. Your PA-radar will be on high alert around your parents, in-laws, friends, and all of those people who feel they have the right to comment on your life (see They).

PAST DUE: A big, freaking, cosmic joke, much like the due date. The good news, however, is that if the 41-week mark is hit and the baby still has not indicated its willingness to leave the Hotel de Mama, your doctor will start talking about inducing labor or scheduling a C-section.

PATERNITY LEAVE: If you're like most men, you have that caveman instinct to provide. "Must. Get. Back. To. Work. Must. Buy. Food. Argh!" This is one of those many times when you will have to curb your natural instincts. Stay home for a week or two at least. Enjoy the time off and try to ease into your new life as a parent and dad. As difficult as it is, it's equally amazing.

PEDIATRICIAN (Selecting): Picking your kid's doctor is a major decision. Obviously, your kid can't weigh in with her concerns and opinions, so it's really about your comfort level with the doctor. You will likely interview a few pediatricians in your search, and you will talk with all kinds of people to get their recommendations. You'll hear that boys should go with male doctors and females with female doctors. You'll hear about a doctor who is like a grandfather. You'll hear about the young, hip new doctor in town. There's only one right pediatrician and that's the one you and your partner like best. And, there's no harm in switching doctors either. Whoever you choose, make sure to ask a lot of questions first and then get all their information to give to the hospital when the baby is born, as your pediatrician may do a neonatal exam right there in the hospital.

PEEING, YOUR PARTNER: As the pregnancy progresses, the baby grows and starts pressing on your partner's bladder. This will result in her having to pee constantly. It will seem like your partner will head to the bathroom to pee, and then on her way back from the bathroom she will need to pee again. Whatever you do, avoid the urge (at all costs) to ask, "Again? Didn't you just go" (see Egg Shells)?

PEE-PEE TEEPEE™: Exclusively for new fathers who have boys, The Pee-Pee TeePee™ is a cover that fits over your newborn's penis while changing his diaper. When the diaper comes off and newborn boys feel the cool air on their little units — they have a tendency to pee. Like an untended fire hose, the little pee-pee will flap all over and send urine flying in all directions. The Pee-Pee TeePee eliminates the need to wear a biohazard suit to avoid the spray. You can also just use a burp cloth to cover his unit during changing.

PENIS, BABY: Every new dad thinks his kid has the biggest baby genitals ever. "Little dude is huge!" As you work your way through your call list, family and friends will ask how your partner is doing and how the kid is. There's a chance the first thing you will tell them is that you think he's going to be hung like a rhino (see Big Genitalia, Circumcision).

PETS: As much as your new kid is a shock to your lifestyle, she is really going to rock your dog (or cat's) world. There are steps that you are encouraged to take prior to bringing home the baby. The pet should no longer have access to whatever is becoming the baby's room. The pet should no longer be allowed on any furniture that the baby will have access to. The introduction of the baby to the pet should be done carefully and by your household's alpha human.

PHOTOS: You will take a lot of them. Tons. Every time the kid so much as moves, you'll get out the cameras (video and still). You will take 100 pictures of the same thing ("Look, she's sleeping in this picture, but her head is tilted to the left instead of the right!"). You won't want to miss anything, and you'll want to document all of it. Your family will constantly ask you for new pictures: "It's been two weeks since our last pictures—we need new ones!" An appropriate response: "It's been two weeks since Baby Jane was born and two weeks since we've slept. So you'll get them when we get around to it!"

PINK (and Blue): Girls wear pink. Boys wear blue. At least that's how it was in 1950. In today's day and age political correctness has taken over. Some parents will dress their boys in pink just to prove a point. Others might only use "neutral" colors like yellow or green. If you are going to avoid using blue or pink with your kid, you forfeit the right to get upset when someone refers to your newborn baby girl as "he."

PLACENTA: Your little angel is crying and being given her APGAR Score. Your wife is fine. You think it's all over. Not quite. Gotta push out the placenta next (see Afterbirth). The placenta is created during pregnancy to nourish the baby, dispose of waste, and generally keep the baby happy and healthy. Your kid is attached to it via the umbilical cord. So, it's good that it's in there—you just don't need to see it coming out. (Some societies consider the placenta a delicacy ... and eat it. Others bury the placenta behind their homes.)

PLACENTA PREVIA: The placenta is supposed to be attached to the upper wall of the uterus. Sometimes it's positioned low and can partially or totally block the cervix. If the mother starts bleeding, both she and the baby can be at risk. As many as one in 15 women experience some level of placenta previa early in their pregnancies. Most often the placenta moves higher in the uterus as the pregnancy progresses.

POOP: It's what you fear most. Beware of the live poop. A classic new parent mistake is changing the diaper before the kid is actually done. Early on, a poop is as much auditory as anything else, and there actually isn't much smell to breastmilk poop. You know how some people sneeze in twos or threes? Well, your baby will probably poop in a similar pattern. Wait to learn the pattern. If you don't, you may be treated to the "live poop" that comes out unexpectedly, its delivery making you think of a frozen yogurt machine's delivery of chocolate-and-banana yogurt (see Opportunity Weight). And you really don't want that. Oh, and just wait until you encounter the mustard-colored yellow stuff with seeds in it (see Seedy Yellow Poop).

PORN: Perhaps during your partner's pregnancy and certainly after, you'll be surfing lots of porn. More than you think. That is, until you see the videos in the baby class, and then you may never want to see a naked woman again (for a while, anyway).

POSTPARTUM DEPRESSION: Despite what a certain male celebrity might think, postpartum depression is a serious illness. Though the exact cause isn't known and it's impossible to predict who will be affected, about 10% of women experience some level of PPD. Pregnancy destroys hormonal balance, and the months following childbirth continue to be hormonally stressful for your partner, so different levels of "baby blues" can be expected. If you notice your partner behaving more strangely than usual, or if she communicates distress to you, always call your pediatrician or her OB/Gyn for advice. Don't wait. There are many things you can do to help alleviate this condition.

POTTIES: You're going to be a dad now. It's time you start talking like one. Your days of "going to the bathroom" or "hitting the head" are over. Following the birth of your kid, you will "go potty."

PRE-ECLAMPSIA: A condition in pregnancy characterized by an abrupt and sharp rise in blood pressure, leakage of large amounts of the protein albumin into the urine, and swelling of the hands, feet, and face. It's another medical term that you don't want to hear when your partner is in her final trimester or after she's checked into the hospital. It's a tremendously serious condition that needs to be monitored carefully (see Eclampsia).

PREGNANCY: If you need to read a definition of pregnancy you simply can't be helped.

PREGNESIA: See Forgetfulness

PRENATAL APPOINTMENT: See Pediatrician

PRENATAL VITAMINS: Your partner will start popping these like a junkie. In order to help the baby's development, she needs to get her daily dose of folic acid, iron and calcium. There are all kinds of prenatal vitamins. Ask the OB/GYN what's best. And if the morning sickness makes her yak them right up, try to get one that does not stink to high heaven, because many pregnant women develop an acute sense of smell that makes them prone to hurling if they get a whiff of anything too strong.

PRIVACY: What privacy? The amount of privacy you have is inversely proportional to the size of your partner's belly. Huge belly = no privacy. By the time she's getting ready to pop, total strangers will have your phone number on their speed dial and feel as if they have the right to comment on your situation.

PUNCTUALITY: The days of quickly gathering your wallet, keys, and sunglasses and jetting out the door to arrive at the dinner party on time are gone. You must now add at least 50 percent more time to your planning.

PUSH: The words you've been waiting (or dreading?) to hear: "It's time to push." This moment is why you went to the baby classes. It's time for the breathing techniques. It's time for the support. It's why your partner has an epidural. One way or another, the baby is coming (see C-Section, Vaginal Delivery). There are two questions people will want to know after the birth: How long was she in labor? And how long did she push? If there is ever a time during labor that your partner will start speaking in tongues, it's while she's pushing (see Ice Chips).

PUSH GIFT: "Honey, I bought you this gift to thank you for being the woman in our relationship so I didn't have to do what you did." Sometimes referred to as a "birthing gift" or "pushing present," it's important that you don't skimp on this. This is not a time for flowers. This is a time for jewelry. And it's not a time for gold-plated anything. We're talking platinum, precious stones, and empty wallets (see Expenses).

QUICKENING: Though it may describe your heart rate, anxiety, or the speed at which your savings is depleting, quickening is the first time your partner feels the baby move (see Kicking).

QUOTES AND CLICHÉS: Pregnancy is like sports in that the "advice" you receive is just so cliché. By the time the kid is actually born, you're likely to tell your relatives, "Yes, the baby is fine. We just took the last 40 weeks one day at a time and just went into that room and gave it our best shot. 100 percent. And, thankfully, everything worked out, but we didn't do it alone..." You know the clichés when you hear them: "Sleep when the baby sleeps." "Get your sleep now." "Dude, you're effed." The 40 weeks leading up to the birth of your child and the months following are just filled with these gems.

RASH: No, not as in the decision to have a kid, but instead as in what your kid is going to get. Your newborn is likely to be born with a rash. And, when that one goes away, there's a good chance she'll get another one. And another. Depending on the level of interest your partner takes in Web sites and other reading materials, these rashes are either common and not to be worried about or a serious, debilitating disease that will not only eat the flesh of your child, but any shag carpet you may have in the house (just kidding). Who has shag carpet anymore (see Diaper Rash).

READING, PARENTS: See Books

READING TO KIDS: (see Books, Children). You must read extensively to your newborn. Otherwise, she might not grow up liking school and you'll only have yourself to blame for the rest of your life.

RECEIVING BLANKETS: Blankets that you will steal from the hospital. Well, since the hospital knows you're going to take them, it's not technically stealing. And since the blankets are free (by virtue of the fact that you have stolen them), they can't have a fancy French name. Fancy French names are only for expensive, big-ticket items (see Bassinette, Layette, Couvades Syndrome). You may wonder about the difference between a receiving blanket and a regular blanket. Good question. Simply, a receiving blanket has the word receiving before the word blanket. A regular blanket doesn't. Hope that clears it up for you (see Swaddle).

REGISTRY: You may have gone through the whole registry exercise when you got married. If you did, you will know that registering has nothing to do with what you think or want. Whether it's a baby registry or wedding registry—the rules are the same. You will end up with a huge amount of stuff that you don't really use or need. And despite your pleas to add a nice plasma TV or new DVD player to the registry—you will, instead, be treated to more baby clothes or another toy that requires assembly, even though you smartly used the "but it's for the kid" argument (see Batteries, Direction).

SCHOOLS: You haven't started looking into preschool yet for your kid? So what if he's not going to be born for another seven months. Get on it! You're behind (see Competition).

SCIATICA: One of the major reasons that your partner will be experiencing lower back pain that may travel into her legs (see Massage). As the baby grows, your partner's internal organs will get shoved all over the place. If the sciatic nerve gets irritated, sciatica results.

SECONDARY INFERTILITY: This refers to the inability to conceive or maintain a pregnancy after having successfully done so before. Secondary infertility is actually pretty common (see Fertility Clinic, Infertility). Since you are a new dad or about to become one, chances are you're not worrying about this right now. You need to get through having the first baby before you start thinking about the next one.

SEEDY YELLOW POOP: (see Diapers, Feedings, Poop). Newborn poop comes in a wide array of colors. There's actually a poop progression that takes place over the first week or so after birth. First comes the black, tarry meconium poop. Then, as breast milk begins to make its way through the baby's body, the poop becomes more of a pasty, brown color, followed by this yellow and seedy poop. If the baby is formula fed, the poop can be pasty or formed and variably colored. The good news is that this predictable color change indicates that your baby is getting enough to eat.

SENSES: You will be amazed at how heightened your partner's senses become when she is pregnant (see Cravings). You can be at work talking on the phone to a (male) colleague about the challenges of pregnancy (for you) and your partner will call on the other line, "I heard that." Never mind that your office is 45 minutes away. Like a dog that hears undetectable-to-human-ears high-pitched sounds, your partner will have physical reactions to all kinds of sounds (and smells) that you can't even detect. And she'll have absolutely no reaction to other smells that you absolutely can detect (see Gas).

SERVANT: It's what you should plan on being during the pregnancy. If your childless friends give you any grief over your lack of participation in the regular poker game, or your giving up your share of the season tickets, just take note: Payback's a bitch.

SEX, AFTER BABY MAKING: The first time you have sex after the kid can be more nerve-wracking than losing your virginity. Your partner may be feeling slightly uneasy about her body, and if she had a vaginal delivery, you may be feeling uneasy about her body, too! (But, you're getting it again—so, just do whatever you have to do in order to close that deal.) Just make sure to be gentle. Oh, yeah, and be careful in other ways, too. It's not like you want to go through this whole pregnancy thing again right away (see Contraception).

SEX, BEFORE MAKING BABY: Remember that sex? Good. Use those images to get you through the next 40 weeks. Oh hell, use those images to get you through the rest of your life.

SEX, DURING PREGNANCY: For men, and specifically their sex lives, being married to a pregnant woman is like having a Ferrari parked in the garage—but you don't have a set of keys so you can't drive it. Here is your already attractive wife in the early/middle stages of pregnancy (second trimester, after the nausea has passed), and she still isn't looking too pregnant to the outside world. Her breasts are getting bigger by the day. She feels bloated and hideous, none of her clothes fit right, and since she doesn't feel sexy, you don't get any. After months with little or no sex already, you're about to explode. She parades about with her new and improved rack, yet she wants nothing to do with sex. It's the ultimate torture, much like the sweet car that you somehow can't drive. In fact, if you bring up the word sex, you'd best get ready for a fight. The conversation might go something like this:

> **HER:** I think it would be great to have two kids.
> **YOU:** Well by the time we get to the point where we can make a second kid, I will have forgotten how to, seeing as how I am completely out of practice in the art of baby-making. Maybe we should go practice now.
> **HER:** Oh, go screw yourself.
> **YOU:** I already planned on it, thanks.

SEX, ORAL: Who are you kidding?

SHAKING: Never, ever shake a baby. Shaking a baby makes the fragile brain bounce back and forth inside the skull, which can cause bruising, swelling, and bleeding, leading to permanent, severe brain damage or death.

SHEA BUTTER CREAM: Thought to help alleviate/avoid stretch marks. You can get it at any number of high-end shops. Also good for the C-section scar.

SHOWERS: After the first few weeks with your newborn, taking a shower will feel like going to a spa. You'll be amazed at how long you can go without taking a shower. When your options are a 10-minute shower or 10 minutes of sleep—you'll inevitably pick the latter. If you go without a shower for too long, however, your friends and family might be less willing to come over and help.

SHOWERS, BABY: Yes, you get a whole bunch of presents, but you also pay the price by being forced to play all kinds of humiliating shower games. There are different kinds of baby showers, but all require you to be on your best behavior. You even need to show up at the "women's only" showers and smile, say thanks, and crack a joke or two to show what a wonderful, invisible partner you are! The couples' showers (which require attendance by both parts of the couple) are a great way to get back at your friends. Since you don't really want to be there, it's only fair that they should have to suffer along with you.

SIDELINE: By holding your baby on its side (like a football), a reflex kicks in, which (hopefully) instantly calms her. She may get so calm, you might want to "do the Heisman" while holding her like this.

SIDS: Sudden Infant Death Syndrome. You can't possibly think of anything more horrible. There are preventative precautions that you can take to reduce the risk of SIDS including: the baby sleeping on her back, keeping the crib free of blankets and other items, and—researched more recently—having her go to sleep with a pacifier.

SINGLETON: It used to be that one baby was the norm. But now with fertility treatments and aging moms who are more likely than younger ones to drop more than one egg at a time increasing the incidence of twins, there is now a term to indicate when there is only one baby in the womb: singleton (See: Multiple Births). All singleton means is that instead of having to buy two of everything at once, you get to buy one of everything. Woo-hoo!

SIPPY CUP: The sippy cup is what your kid will drink from when she is old enough. It's a magical cup that she can throw on the floor (repeatedly) and it won't spill any of the water, juice, or other contents. It also won't break, which is key. The sippy cup, for some reason, seems to react more violently with gravity than most objects. There's no other explanation for the reason why it's always on the floor.

SLEEP BANKING: If you had the opportunity to collect a dollar for your future kid's college fund for every person that tells you to "get your sleep now, because once the kid comes, you won't be getting any," you would likely be able to send your kid to an Ivy League school—and have enough left over to retire and travel around the world. Go ahead and laugh the first couple of times you're told this and act like it's new information. Then, try not to throttle the messenger (see Quotes & Clichés).

SLEEP DEPRIVATION: It's no joke: You will not get any sleep. You will be cranky. Confused. Forgetful (see Pregnesia). And loopy. After the first couple of weeks, you'll be sure you can handle it. Two weeks becomes three, which becomes four, five, and six. Before long, you forget to shower. You forget to shave. You forget your name. You'll be amazed how refreshing an hour of uninterrupted sleep can be. You'll learn to nap in any situation (including while standing in line at your local deli). While you will get to a point of wanting to kill the next person that tells you that you need to "get your sleep now," it's the truth. The time will come when your kid does finally start sleeping through the night—and you'll feel like you just won the lottery.

"SLEEP WHEN THE BABY SLEEPS": Another genius piece of advice. And it would be a good one if you, like the baby, only had to worry about eating, sleeping, and crapping in your diaper (that day will come again for you in a few years). But since you have a number of other responsibilities and pesky annoyances like work, shopping for food, walking the dog, taking out the trash and dirty diapers (recommended daily), and generally keeping your world from imploding, this advice is pretty useless for you—which does not mean that you cannot use it on your partner to show what a giving guy you are.

SLEEPING: Probably what you want more than anything. You'll trade your most prized possession for an extra hour of sleep.

SLEEPING, BABY: Probably what you want more than even the previous entry. You'll trade your most prized possession for your baby to sleep an extra hour.

SLEEP CONSULTANT: Being a parent will introduce you to an entirely new category of professional advisors. A good one is worth every penny. The "sleep consultant" is one of them (see Lactation Consultant). The sleep consultant is an expert in helping you train your baby to sleep. Sort of like a golf coach helping you with your game. The sleep consultant will likely tell you that all the things you're doing are wrong, but if you listen to her, you could be rewarded with hours and hours of uninterrupted sleep (see Colic).

SLING: (see BabyBjörn). The sling is a less-complicated, baby-carrying contraption than the Björn.

SNOOGLE™: It's like having another body in bed with you. Or has been described as sleeping with an anaconda between you and your partner. The Snoogle™ is an enormous pillow that has two purposes. First, it is designed to allow your partner to sleep more comfortably. The shape allows for her to sleep on her side with the pillow supporting her belly. Second, it is designed to make you as uncomfortable as possible sharing the bed with her. It's sort of payback for not being able to carry the kid. The Snoogle is a remarkably comfortable pillow. Try to avoid the urge to take it from your partner. She may also be given more than one. You will not be allowed to use the extra Snoogle. You know how "Trix are for kids"? Snoogles are for pregnant women.

SNORING: Just as you might be surprised to hear your partner burp or fart, you'll be scared when you hear her snore. This is not the sweet, gentle, peaceful breathing and cute snoring you may have heard over the years. You will wake up in a panic wondering what happened to your partner. Where is she and how did you end up in bed with this man? Then you'll realize that the horrific sounds are actually coming from your wife. Best to just grab a pillow and head for another room. It's your only hope. And pray your neighbors don't call the humane society.

SOOTHIES®: Chilled pads that your partner might use to help soothe and heal breastfeeding damage. Soothies help heal cracked, bleeding nipples.

SPECIAL MEAL: On the eve of your discharge from the hospital, you may get to order a special meal. Just remember, your "special meal" is still cooked in a hospital kitchen by hospital cooks. So while you may order the steak, don't expect the kind of steak you are probably thinking about. In fact, don't order the steak. It may put you off steak forever.

SPIT-UP: Like the whole poop thing, spit-up is another baby bodily function that you can count on. After each meal, you'll need to burp your baby (see Burping). With the burping often comes half the meal. Babies also have some kind of innate sense that tells them the shirt you're wearing is expensive and has just been dry-cleaned.

SPORTS: If you are a sports fan and watch quite a bit of your favorite team, you might want to get used to not watching quite a bit of your favorite team. Or you might want to make sure your TiVo is working so you can watch the games while your partner sleeps. If you're smart, however, you can "volunteer" to watch the baby, feed her, and change her during the game. That way, you get huge points for proactively helping and still get to see your game.

SPRAYING: See Pee-Pee TeePee™

STATION: You're likely to hear the doctor tell your partner that the baby is at [insert number here] station. You'll be confused. Sure, you learned what this meant in baby class, but now that your partner is in the delivery room—who remembers anything about the baby class? Station is a rating from −3 to +4 that describes the position of the baby in pelvis. Minus-three is a "floating baby," zero means the head has engaged in the pelvis, and plus-four is crowning.

STORK: After experiencing birth the real way, you may wish that the kid were actually delivered by a stork.

STRETCH MARKS: Your partner may experience some marks on her stomach, hips, legs, and breasts—and you would too if your body were being stretched by having a kid grow inside you (see Shea Butter Cream).

STROLLERS: Shopping for a stroller is like shopping for a car. You will test drive the stroller by wheeling it around the store—taking tight turns, running over obstacles, and creating a driving course around displays. Like a car, the stroller you buy is as much a status symbol as anything else (see Baby Gear). It's the first thing you'll notice when another family strolls by. You'll whisper with envy if they have a more expensive model, and you'll silently mock them if they have the cheap equivalent. It's important to buy the right stroller for your lifestyle. And you don't just need one. You'll need multiple strollers depending on the situation and age (weight, height) of your kid(s).

STROLLER, BUGABOO™: The Bugaboo is the gold-standard of strollers. It's the Ferrari. Parents who push their kid around in a Bugaboo seem to be walking on air, or in slow motion. You may instinctively stop and enviously stare as they walk by. Any description of the Bugaboo is usually followed up by "Didja know that [insert celebrity name here] uses one for her kid, [insert weird name here]?"

STROLLER, JOGGER: If you are into your exercise and like to hike, walk or run, a jogger is the ideal way to include your kid in your regimen (see Baby Gear).

STROLLER, UMBRELLA: It's a lightweight, easy-to-carry, easy-to-breakdown, inexpensive stroller that is ideal for traveling and crowded malls (see Baby Gear).

SUCKING: There is quite a bit of sucking associated with being a new parent. Your newborn will be sucking on breasts, pacifiers, fingers, bottles, and the air. In fact, you and your partner will get a good laugh out of the fact that your baby will likely suck in her sleep; it's the equivalent of baby air-guitar.

SUSHI: If you love it, you're gonna miss it. Well, technically you can eat it, but your partner can't (see Alcohol). Which means that you'd better not. At least not in front of her.

SWADDLE: Something you will learn about in your baby class (and another pregnancy/baby-related term that means something simple, but needs a fancy name). Though it seems to border on cruel, many kids actually sleep better if they are tightly wrapped up in a blanket, much like a human burrito. You will be taught how to pin his arms down and legs up while basically rendering him totally helpless (okay, even more helpless). You will feel like you're hurting the kid until 1) you understand that he likes this feeling because it reminds him of being back on the "inside," and 2) you will get more sleep if he's wrapped tightly. And, you want more sleep. There are swaddle-specific blankets you can buy (which is like buying pancake mix), but there is great pride to make your baby's swaddling from scratch!

SWING: Also known as magical. Imagine, if you will: Your baby is wailing and just won't stop; you put her in the swing and she stops. In order to successfully care for a baby, you sometimes need to think like a baby. Evidently, the swing replicates some of the movement that the baby experienced for the 40 weeks on the inside. Movement oftentimes makes her go to sleep (which is why so many parents will drive around in their cars to get their babies to sleep). Like everything in baby land, there are huge number of different models from which to choose. Some have music and flashing lights (see Batteries). Some have up to 10 speeds. Some are more basic. You just have to make the right choice based on your budget and available space (some are huge!). But, there are certain purchases you don't want to make based solely on price (like the cheapest motorcycle helmet, for example). Sometimes, it's best to go high-end, as the reward (in the case of the swing) could be more sleep.

SYMPATHY WEIGHT: (see also Opportunity Weight). Your partner is likely to gain anywhere from 30–60 pounds, depending on a whole slew of variables (see Bed Rest, Cravings, Multiple Births). Men are likely prepared for this. What they may not be prepared for is the fact that many men also gain around 15 pounds during the pregnancy. This weight gain is more likely the result of "opportunity" than "sympathy." During pregnancy, men have the opportunity to partake in their partner's cravings and cut back on their workouts ("But honey, I'd rather take a slow walk around the block with you!"). After 40 weeks of this behavior, many men also feel ready to give birth.

TEA, MOTHER'S MILK: A special tea that helps with the production of mother's breast milk (see Fenugreek). Check with your doctor before your partner ingests any herbal, homeopathic, or supplemental vitamins, nutrients, or concoctions as they can be upsetting to baby's stomach and can interact with other substances.

TEETHING: You've probably heard of teething. The first tooth usually comes around six months, more or less. It's a painful experience for your baby as her teeth start to come in. Her gums will be tremendously sore, and she'll need to suck on cold teething rings, chilled pacifiers, or a rawhide bone. (Sorry, that's when a dog is teething; it's the sleep deprivation.) Teething sometimes results in a low-grade fever. You will feel helpless, as sometimes teething can occur for months before the teeth come in. Teething is also accompanied by significant drooling. And no, giving your baby a sip of port is not an option.

TELEVISION (in Hospital): Hospital televisions, like the food and the cots, leave a little something to be desired. But, for once, that's okay. Because you won't have any control over the remote anyway. The controls of the TV are very much in your partner's control. You might try to turn it on to watch a game or your favorite show, but if that game or show doesn't interest your partner, don't bother. There aren't any battles to pick at this point, so you're better off just repressing the urge. If your kid is being born on Super Bowl Sunday or during the NCAA Championships, you have nobody to blame but yourself. You should have planned better. There are Web sites you could have consulted to learn the possible due dates of your kid if you and your partner conceive on that day. Long story short—better off just ignoring the fact that you have a TV in your room (and figure out which rooms around you are empty).

THE FIVE S's: (see DVD: *Happiest Baby on the Block*). Shhhhhhing, Swaddling, Swaying, Sideline, and Sucking. Also referred to as "baby voodoo." If you don't know the five S's before your kid is born, you have nobody to blame but yourself.

THERMOMETER: There are all sorts of ways to take your baby's temperature. There are oral, armpit, ear, and rectal thermometers. It may be some sort of cosmic joke that the rectal thermometer gives you the most accurate temperature reading.

THEY: The absolute bane of your existence. "They" will constantly be telling you what to do (see Advice, Unsolicited). "They" will weigh in with their thoughts on your baby's name. "They" will tell you how to treat your partner. "They" will find it okay to rub your partner's belly without first asking. "They" will tell you that you need to sell your motorcycle (if applicable) because "you're a dad now." The problem is that in many cases, you don't even know who "they" are. "They" are strangers you meet in the store or on the street. "They" are other parents who just think that "you're doing it wrong." "They" will drive you insane.

THRUSH: Sometimes, the mother catches a fungal infection called thrush while breastfeeding and passes it on to the baby through her breast. Then the baby passes it back to the mother. And the two of them become these toxic partners in symbiosis (see Mastitis). Call the doctor at the first sign of white patches in the baby's mouth or if your partner complains of unusual and painful physical sensations when breastfeeding.

TO FIND OUT OR NOT TO FIND OUT: (See Gender)

TOXEMIA: See Pre-Eclampsia

TOYS: You will buy them. You will buy lots of them. More will be given to you by friends and family (see Registry). But the kid will shun all of them just to rip up a magazine article that you hadn't finished reading. The good news is that you get to play with all of these toys as well and there are some cool ones (see Batteries). This is a precursor to the first video game console you buy for him (PlayStation 18 by that time) with the caveat that "it's for him." Yeah, sure it is.

TRAVEL: Just because you have a kid doesn't mean you have to stop traveling. It simply means that the amount of luggage you need to bring with you has increased by a factor of infinity. There are toys, clothes, bouncy seats, travel cribs, hundreds of diapers, wipes, and more—and that's if you're staying in a developed country. Your little baby who is all of three weeks old will require more stuff for your trip than you and your partner combined. It's shocking.

TRIMESTER, FIRST: Approximately three months duration. This can go any number of ways (see Morning Sickness). Regardless of whether or not your partner has morning sickness, she is definitely going to be exhausted as her body adjusts to the alien being living inside of her. During the first trimester, your partner will be tired. Very, very tired. She will likely want to sleep all the time. Her body is changing. Her friends will tell her that she's glowing. She will just feel sore and bloated. Try to avoid phrases like, "Wow! You're really showing!" Women just aren't that fond of gaining weight—even if there's a baby growing inside of them.

TRIMESTER, SECOND: Approximately three months duration. This is the honeymoon trimester for your partner (and therefore you). In most cases, any morning sickness has gone away. You partner isn't feeling too big. And, like a light switch turning on—her energy comes back. If there were ever a trimester where you might get some, this is the one.

TRIMESTER, THIRD: Approximately three months duration. The honeymoon is over. Your partner is starting to feel huge. The hormones are kicking in big time. She's likely peeing all the time, and there's a good chance that she's having trouble sleeping (see Snoogle). The nesting instinct will kick in fast and furious during the third trimester. You will find yourself becoming quite familiar with any number of baby stores and probably mired in a myriad of home improvement projects (see Baby's Room).

TRIMESTER, FOURTH: What the &%*#? Four trimesters? The first three months of your kid's life (see Due Date, Weeks) are really the fourth trimester. During this time, your kid is in shock, which is why she cries so much and requires support and attention (see Noise Machine, Sucking, Swaddle).

TUMMY-TIME: After your baby is born, you will need to spend at least 30 minutes a day doing tummy-time. This is simply having the baby on her tummy. It's important to do, as it helps the kid develop the muscles in his arms and neck. Chances are your baby will hate tummy-time.

U

ULTRASOUND: A serious reality check. Each time you get to see updated images of your kid growing, or hear her heartbeat, you will be reminded that your life is about to take a dramatic turn. If you aren't particularly religious or spiritual, the first ultrasound may be the closest you come to believing in a God (pick one).

ULTRASOUND PICTURES: Amazing for you and your partner (see Fear). Fodder for your relatives. Exciting for your partner's friends. And a source of feigned excitement for your (male) friends. If you are able to make out an actual kid in the ultrasound picture, it's kind of cool. Depending on when the first one is taken, your kid may look more like a form in the Rorschach test then it does a human form. You will gush over this picture. Your parents and in-laws may have wallet-sized copies made and laminated. Each time you get a new ultrasound picture, the kid looks more and more like a … kid, in an X-ray, boney, alien, almost-human kinda way. Ultrasound pictures make the whole expectant dad thing get more and more real (see Fear).

UMBILICAL CORD: The cord that connects your developing kid with the placenta and keeps your kid nourished and living in a clean environment. After the birth, you'll have a chance to cut the cord. Its residual tip forms the bellybutton. The thing sorta looks like a beer bong, which could very well explain the fact that years from now your kid will be in his college dorm eagerly grabbing the tube and begging to be fed liquid hops and barley. It'll feel like coming home.

UMBILICAL CORD STUMP: After the cord is cut, it is clamped. After 10 days, or up to a month or so, the clamped part will die, and it will just fall off. It's a nice memento for the scrapbook, dontcha think?

UTERUS: It's where your kid is living for those 40 weeks (plus/ minus). It's a nice, comfortable home. And though the kid doesn't have a whole lot of room to stretch out (see Kicking), she does get an all-she-can-eat-buffet (see Umbilical Cord), five-star accommodations, and a quiet place to sleep whenever she wants. Plus there are no bills to pay (see Expenses), tests to take, or chores to do. Uterus may come from the Latin meaning: Utopia.

offthemark.com

VACCINATIONS: It may not come as a big surprise that the decision whether or not to vaccinate your newborn child comes with controversy. And it may come as no surprise that both sides of the controversy are vocal and aggressive. There are those that believe vaccinating is unnecessary and wrong. Those that take this side will point to studies that they believe show that vaccinations may lead to an increase in autism. Those that argue for vaccinations make their case on the fact that the new vaccinations don't have the levels of lead that old ones had and blah, blah, blah. Just ask your doctor.

VAGINAL DELIVERY: This is the "normal" way for a baby to be born. Not sure what's so normal about it, though.

VAGINAL REJUVENATION: Women (and men) get face-lifts, liposuction, breast augmentations, and other surgeries designed to make them stay "younger" longer. The latest fad (for women) is called vaginal rejuvenation, a procedure that involves tightening the vagina with a few well-placed stitches.

VARICOSE VEINS: Not just for old people anymore and more fun for your partner! Varicose veins, or the bulging/swelling of veins, occur when veins (in this case particularly in the legs) fail to properly circulate blood. If you consider what's going on internally and the fact that the baby is pushing around all of your partner's internal organs, it's somewhat easy to understand how her body and her veins might react by freaking out. Eating well and continuing to exercise during pregnancy can help alleviate varicose veins.

VBAC: Vaginal Birth After C-Section. This is best described as a ... ummm ... vaginal birth after having had a C-section the last time you had a baby.

VIDEOS, IN CLASS: The purpose of the baby classes is to prepare you for the baby. So it makes perfect sense to watch a video or two. But it's a shock to actually watch the various births. You will wonder who these people are and why they have agreed to let cameras record everything (Every. Thing.). You might think that they are receiving free medical care or millions of dollars. Why else would they do this? Nope. It's all for the good of humanity. It's so people like you can get skeeved out watching their experiences (see Baby Classes).

APRIL FOOLS DAY IN
THE MATERNITY WARD

WALKING: Something you will or should do a whole lot of for the health of your partner, the baby, and you.

WALKING THE HALLS: If your partner isn't dilated enough to be checked into the hospital, the nurses may ask you if you want to "walk the halls" for an hour. Exercise helps the dilation process. Of course, the reason that you're at the hospital in the first place is because your partner is in labor and is having intense, painful contractions. So walking the halls isn't exactly a leisurely stroll. It's a slow, waddling trek that is routinely interrupted by knee-buckling pain and shrieks of anguish (for your partner, too).

WATER BREAKING: Also known as: Ruptured membranes. This is that scene that you fully expect but rarely happens: You're at a restaurant with your partner who is 39 weeks pregnant when her water breaks. There's a frenzied panic as you try to get your wife out of the room to the car to begin the race across town to the hospital. Fact is that only 15% of women really experience their water breaking. The rest of the time, the membranes are ruptured by the doctor (with a thing that looks like a crochet needle with a hook on the end. Again, be glad it's not you). In order to preserve your leather seats, you might think of having towels in your car during the last few weeks of her pregnancy.

WEEKS: The new measurement of your life. Prior to pregnancy, you most likely defined time in terms of days, weeks, months, or years, but now it's all about the weeks and months. The baby isn't four months old; she's 17 weeks. Your partner isn't seven months pregnant; she's 29 weeks. You've never spent so much effort in your life describing time in terms of weeks. (After a while, weeks will morph to months. Your baby isn't 2 years old; she's 24 months.) You may fight this for a while and use appropriate terms like, a month and a half (for 6 weeks), but you will lose that battle.

WHITE NOISE: For more than nine months, your baby listened to the wonderful (and extremely loud) internal stylings of your partner's heartbeat and blood flow. As a result, when your kid is born, you might consider buying a white noise machine that offers sounds like rain, the ocean, or a waterfall. This may help your baby fall asleep. (And, frankly, anything that may help your baby sleep is worth the investment.) In emergencies, running water or television static may soothe your baby (see Noise Machine).

WIFE: (If applicable.) After this experience, if you don't think she's the most amazing person on the planet, you should be shot. Chances are she put you through some tough experiences leading up to the birth (which isn't about to stop), but if you actually think about all the things that are happening to her body (or read about them) and then realize that she did all of this while still doing all the other things she does, well then, you have no choice but to be amazed. Tell her. Show her.

WILLS: This not about the "battle of the wills." (What purpose would it serve to discuss that? You lose.) Instead, this is about the kind of Will you create in order to distribute your assets when you die. There's a good chance that having a Will isn't something to which you've given much thought (see Insurance, Life). Now that you're having a kid, it's something to consider.

WIPES: Just what it sounds like. You will also use them to clean her hands or her face from time to time, but the main use is to wipe the little baby butt. Early on you will probably use 10 or 20 times the number of wipes that you actually need for fear of getting any poop on you. After your hundredth or thousandth diaper change, however, you will become more economical in your wipe usage (see Expenses). Unless there's a blow-out. In that case feel free to use whatever it takes to get the job done, including a hose.

WIPES WARMER: Believe it or not, there is such a thing as a wipes warmer. It's a box in which the wipes are placed that will keep the wipes warm. Why? Well, you don't want your poor little baby to have his butt cleaned with a cold wipe, do you? It needs to be slightly warmed like good Brie cheese. This will allow for maximum comfort for your kid and provide fodder for an argument in the future when your kid tells you that he hates you and that you don't love him. "Don't love you? When you were a baby, we bought a freaking wipes warmer so you wouldn't suffer the shock and dismay of having your butt cleaned with a room temperature wipe! Don't tell me I don't love you! Now, get back inside and clean your room, or I'll be forced to ice the toilet paper as retribution!"

WORK: The most difficult part of the whole new dad thing is the fact that you will most likely have to go back to work at some point. And if dealing at home isn't bad enough when you're sleep deprived, dealing with co-workers, bosses, and clients is that much worse. Fortunately, most of your professional dealings

will be with understanding people who "have been there" or who at least think they have an inkling of what you're going through. Of course, you'll have to deal with the never-ending snickers, points, and snide questions from the a**hole that sits in the office next to you. "Hey Bob, get much sleep last night?" You could choose to kill him or instead just take mental notes and plot something more devious. You see, this is where sleep deprivation actually becomes a good thing. Sleeping only two or three hours a night for weeks on end is the only time that your brain likely becomes twisted enough to imagine the sorts of things you might do to your annoying colleague—and consider carrying them out.

ZIP PDQ! (Pretty Darn Quick!): Zip up your pants! Remember this from sixth grade? No? Well, trust me, it was hilarious back in the day. Plus, I couldn't think of any other entries. That means you're done!

Finally, here is a map of the human brain and what you have to look forward to:

First, your brain:

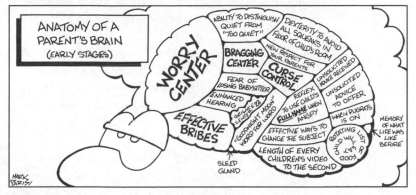

Then, your kid's:

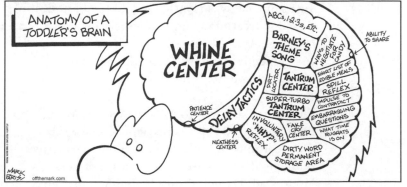

Acknowledgments

Perhaps it's a bit cart-before-the-horse to work on the thank-you speech before the book is even published, but the fact is I've been thinking about having the opportunity to write this very piece for longer than it took to write this book.

For as long as I can remember, I've wanted to be a writer. Not simply just a writer, but an I-make-my-living-by-my-writing type of writer. And I've always wanted to write a book. I've written and written and written for so many years, but I've never been able to figure out what "the book" was going to be. That is, I wasn't able to figure it out until my son, Kolby, came into the world. Turns out, I couldn't just be a writer. I first needed to be a dad.

There are many people that I must thank. And since I don't have to worry about being rushed off the stage as the band starts to play some theme song from "name that movie," I will try to mention them all.

This project would not have happened without the mentoring of my friend, editor, agent, and at times, therapist, Lisa Rojany Buccieri. For nearly 20 years she has been telling me that I have a book in me. Turns out she was right. She read the first draft of the book treatment and helped it grow into a proper proposal. And she edited many drafts of the book... and helped it grow into something worthy of a bookstore bookshelf.

Thanks are also due to Amanda Weiler, M.D., who carefully vetted this manuscript to make sure the medical terminology was on the mark. Any subsequent errors are all my fault, not hers. Mom, Dad, Daniel, Susie, Joelle, Arthur, Felix,

Susan, Marc, and Natacha: You are nearest and dear to me, and have always pushed me to succeed. (Sometimes with overt support—and other times by pissing me off and lighting an, "I'll show them" fire under my butt.) The truth is my family (like so many others) is strange. All of the people listed above are strange in their own, unique ways. We have our laughs and we have had our share of battles. But somehow we manage to find a way to be there for each other when it really counts—and, more importantly, many more times when it doesn't.

My father-in-law likes to say, "Youth is wasted on the young." Perhaps the problem is that when we get older we forget about our dreams. I'm not talking about goals. I'm talking about dreams. We forget what we "wanted to be when we grow up." And we stop making those (big) dreams come true. The flipside is that when we're young, we dream and dream and dream, but don't often have the means, drive, or support to make them come true. And, that, perhaps, is the waste.

Yet here I am, living proof that an old dog can, in fact, learn new tricks. No more will I have to say, "Well, if I can do anything ... I'd write." Instead, I'm simply going to do it. And I have all the inspiration I need. So, finally, to my wife, Lisa, my son, Kolby, (okay, and my dog, Harley), I thank you for the means, the drive, and most of all, the support that has created a universe in which this day has been allowed to materialize. This book would not have been possible without you. And, in turn, I promise to provide the means, drive, and support to help you find your own way and forever be in a position to chase and achieve your own dreams.

Index

Advice, Unsolicited ... 4

Afterbirth ... 5

Alcohol/Wine ... 5

Allergies ... 5, 6

Amniocentesis ... 6

Amniotic Fluid ... 6

Anaphylaxis ... 5, 6

Announcements ... 6, 7

APGAR Score ... 2, 7, 27

Aspirator ... 7

Au Pair ... 7

BabyBjörn ... 8

Baby Blues ... 8

Baby Breast Buds ... 8

Baby Classes ... 9, 20, 65

Baby Food ... 9

Baby Gear ... 9, 25, 32, 35, 36, 49, 97

Baby Proofing ... 10

Babysitters ... 10, 51

Baby Talk, Babies ... 10

Baby Talk, Parents ... 11

Baby's Room ... 11

Baby-centered Web sites ... 11

Back Labor ... 12

Bassinette ... 12

Batteries ... 12, 61

Bed Rest ... 12, 54

Bib ... 13

Big Baby Stores ... 13

Big Genitalia ... 13, 83

Birth Canal ... 13, 27, 37

Birth Coach ... 15

Birthmark ... 15

Birth Weight ... 15

Birthing Gift ... 86

Birthing Room ... 15, 57

Blood ... 16, 107

Bloody Show ... 16, 71

Blue (and Pink) ... 16, 83

Bonding ... 16, 18, 46

Books, Children's Books ... 17

Books, *The Girlfriends' Guide
to Pregnancy* ... 17

Boppy/Nursing Pillow ... 17, 72

Bottle-Feeding ... 18

Botulism ... 18, 55

Bouncy Seat ... 12, 18

Breastfeeding ... 9, 18, 20, 40, 46,
        64, 65, 72, 75

Breastfeeding, in public ... 19

Breast Milk ... 9, 18, 19, 26, 27,
        66, 78, 100

Breast Pump ... 19

Breasts, Engorged ... 19

Breasts, Off-Limits and Sore ... 20

Breathing ... 6, 20

Breech ... 20

Burp Cloth ... 21, 36, 66, 82

Burping ... 21, 47, 96

Caesarian (C-Section) ... 23

Call List ... 24, 39

Car Seat ... 24, 25, 26

Carpal Tunnel Syndrome ... 24

Cars ... 25, 39

Changing Pad ... 21, 25, 36

Changing Table ... 11, 25, 70

Checking Out of Hospital ... 25

Circumcision ... 26, 83

Colic ... 26, 32, 95

Colostrum ... 18, 26

Competition ... 27, 66

Conception ... 27

Conehead ... 13, 27

Constipation ... 27

Contraception ... 27, 91

Contractions ... 29, 65, 71, 108

Contractions, Braxton-Hicks ... 29

Cooing ... 10, 29

Cooler, Thermal ... 29

Cord blood ... 30

Cot ... 30

Couvades Syndrome ... 31

Cracked Nipples ... 31, 65

Cradle Cap ... 31

Cravings ... 31, 98

Crib ... 32, 70, 80, 93

Crowning ... 32, 96

Crying, Baby ... 32

Crying, Wife or Partner ... 33

Cutting the Cord ... 33

CVS (Chronic Villus Sampling) ... 6, 33

Dad/Father ... 24, 33, 34, 44, 61, 110

Date Night ... 34

Diaper ... 35

Diaper Bag ... 25, 36, 66

Diaper Pail ... 36

Diaper Rash ... 36, 88

Diapers, Cloth ... 35, 36

Diapers, Dirty ... 36

Diapers, Disposable ... 35, 37

Diet/Nutrition ... 37

Dilation ... 37, 38, 41, 65, 108

Directions, Reading ... 38

Doctor's Appointments ... 38

Doula ... 38

Driving ... 39, 56

Dr. Harvey Karp ... 39

Due Date ... 39, 75, 81

Eating, Baby ... 40, 46

Eating, Parents ... 40

Eclampsia ... 41, 85, 102

Ectopic Pregnancy ... 41

Edema ... 41

Effacement ... 41, 65

Egg Shells ... 42, 56, 82

Embolism ... 42

Engorgement ... 19, 20, 42

Epidural ... 42, 57, 65, 86

Episiotomy ... 42

Exercise ... 38, 43, 49, 97, 107

Expenses ... 43

False Labor ... 29, 44, 48

Family ... 4, 24, 51, 83

Fear ... 44, 66

Feedings ... 18, 40, 45, 74

Fenugreek ... 45, 100

Fertility Clinic ... 45, 60, 89

Fingers and Toes ... 45, 48

Food Intolerances ... 5, 45

Fontanel ... 45

Food In, Food Out ... 45

Forceps ... 46

Forgetfulness ... 46

Formula ... 9, 19, 36, 46, 78, 91

Free Time ... 46

Gas, Baby ... 47

Gas, Wife ... 21, 47

Gender, Finding Out ... 6, 48

Gestational Diabetes ... 48, 49

Getting Sent Home ... 48

Gifts ... 48

Glider ... 49

Glucose Screen ... 49

Glucose Tolerance Test ... 48, 49

Golf ... 16, 43, 51, 54

Grandparents ... 51

Grocery Shopping ... 51

Hand Sanitizer / Hand Washing ... 52

Heartbeat ... 38, 53, 70, 104, 109

Heating Pad ... 53

Hell Night ... 53, 74

Hemorrhoids ... 53

Hiccups ... 53

High Chair ... 54

High or Low ... 54

High-Risk Pregnancy ... 54

Hobbies ... 54

Hole in the Head ... 27, 45, 54

Home Birth ... 15, 55

Honey ... 55

Hormones ... 13, 32, 33, 42, 49,
                56, 103

Hospital, Route To ... 56

Hospital, Tour ... 57

Humidifier ... 57

Hurl ... 57

Hyperemesis ... 58

Hypochondria ... 58, 61

Ice Chips ... 59, 86

Incontinence ... 60, 63

Incompetent Cervix ... 59, 69

Inducing ... 60, 64, 81

Infertility ... 60

In-Laws ... 6, 9, 15, 60, 73

Insurance, Health ... 60

Insurance, Life ... 7, 60

Internet ... 7, 58, 61

Invisible ... 61

iPod ... 9, 61

It Is What It Is ... 61, 71

Jamberry ... 17

Jealousy ... 62

Jumper ... 62

Kegels ... 63

Kicking ... 63

La Leche League International ... 64

Labor ... 9, 23, 48, 57, 60, 64, 74

Labor Plan ... 65, 81

Lactation Consultant ... 65, 95

Lamaze ... 9, 15, 20

Latch ... 65

Layette ... 66

Leaving the House ... 66

Length ... 66

Letdown Reflex ... 18, 66

Leucorrhea ... 67

Mannary Glands ... 68

Massage ... 9, 15, 68

Mastitis ... 31, 69

Maternity Clothes ... 69

Meconium Poop ... 69, 91

Midwives ... 38, 68

Miscarriages ... 59, 69

Mobiles ... 70

Monitors, Baby ... 70

Monitors, Fetal ... 70

Mood Swings ... 56, 71

Morning Sickness ... 71, 85, 102, 103

Morphine ... 71

Mucous Plug ... 16, 65, 71

Multiple Births ... 71

My Brest Friend ... 72

Names ... 4, 73

Nanny ... 7, 73

Narcotics ... 9, 74

Natural Birth ... 42, 74

Nesting ... 74, 103

Night Nurse ... 74

Nine Months ... 74, 109

Nipple Confusion ... 9, 75, 80

Nipple Cream ... 75

Nipple Shield ... 18, 75

Noise Machine ... 75, 109

Non-Stress Test (NST) ... 75

Nursery ... 11, 53, 76

Nurses ... 26, 65, 76

Nursing Bra ... 20, 76

OB/GYN ... 27, 39, 77, 85

"On a Scale of 1–10" ... 77

Onesie ... 77

Operating Room ... 15, 21, 23, 77

Opportunity Weight ... 78

Ounces ... 78

Pacifier ... 76, 80

Pack 'n Play ... 25, 70, 80

Paint Chips/Colors ... 81

Paperwork ... 81

Parenting Magazines ... 81

Parents ... 81

Passive Aggressiveness ... 81

Past Due ... 81

Paternity Leave ... 82

Pediatrician (Selecting) ... 82

Peeing, Your Partner ... 82

Pee-Pee TeePee ... 37, 82, 96

Penis, Baby ... 83

Pets ... 54, 83

Photos ... 83

Pink (and Blue) ... 83

Placenta ... 5, 33, 83, 105

Placenta Previa ... 84

Poop ... 36, 37, 61, 84

Postpartum Depression ... 8, 33, 84

Potties ... 85

Pre-Eclampsia ... 41, 85, 102

Pregnancy ... 12, 27, 33, 41, 42,
48, 54, 60, 69, 85,
92, 99

Pregnesia ... 46, 85

Prenatal Appointment ... 85

Prenatal Vitamins ... 85

Privacy ... 85

Punctuality ... 86

Push ... 83, 86

Push Gift ... 86

Quickening ... 87

Quotes & Clichés ... 87

Rash ... 88

Reading, Parents ... 88

Reading to Kids ... 88

Receiving Blankets ... 66, 88

Registry ... 88

Schools ... 89

Sciatica ... 89

Secondary Infertility ... 89

Seedy Yellow Poop ... 91

Senses ... 81, 91

Servant ... 91

Sex, After Baby Making ... 91

Sex, Before Making Baby ... 91

Sex, During Pregnancy ... 92

Sex, Oral ... 92

Shaking ... 92

Shea Butter Cream ... 92

Showers ... 92

Showers, Baby ... 93

Sideline ... 62, 93, 101

SIDS (Sudden Infant Death
    Syndrome) ... 80, 93

Singleton ... 93

Sippy Cup ... 93

Sleep Banking ... 94

Sleep Deprivation ... 46, 94, 111

Sleep When the Baby Sleeps ... 87, 94

Sleeping ... 11, 44, 49, 91, 92, 93,
    101, 111

Sleeping, Baby ... 94

Sling ... 95

Snoogle ... 95

Snoring ... 95

Soothies ... 96

Special Meal ... 96

Spit-Up ... 96

Sports ... 96

Spraying ... 96

Station ... 96

Stork ... 96

Stretch Marks ... 97

Strollers ... 97

Stroller, Bugaboo ... 97

Stroller, Jogger ... 97

Stroller, Umbrella ... 97

Sucking ... 19, 75, 80, 97

Sushi ... 98

Swaddle ... 98

Swing ... 98

Sympathy Weight ... 32, 98

Tea, Mother's Milk ... 100

Teething ... 100

Television (in Hospital) ... 101

The Five S's ... 101

Thermometer ... 101

They ... 101

Thrush ... 102

To Find Out or Not To Find Out ... 48

Toxemia ... 102

Toys ... 102

Travel ... 25, 102

Trimester, First ... 102

Trimester, Fourth ... 103

Trimester, Second ... 103

Trimester, Third ... 103

Tummy-Time ... 103

Ultrasound ... 38, 104, 105

Ultrasound Pictures ... 38, 104, 105

Umbilical Cord ... 30, 33, 105

Umbilical Cord Stump ... 105

Uterus ... 13, 23, 41, 105

Vaccinations ... 106

Vaginal Delivery ... 74, 106

Vaginal Rejuvenation ... 106

Varicose Veins ... 107

VBAC (Vaginal Birth
    After C-Section) ... 107

Videos, In Class ... 107

Vomiting ... 41, 57, 58

Walking ... 10, 43, 97, 108

Walking the Halls ... 108

Water Breaking ... 65, 108

Weeks ... 6, 33, 39, 45, 49, 70,
    74, 109

White Noise ... 75, 109

Wife ... 33, 56, 109

Wills ... 110

Wipes ... 36, 69, 102, 110

Wipes Warmer ... 110

Work ... 81, 110

Notes